Praise for the Work of H. L. Hix

About *Surely As Birds Fly*

"... every word is alive and at work on the page, contributing to a book that is beautiful, frightening, cerebral and visceral." —THE KANSAS CITY STAR

"Tabloid violence, complicated theology and lines of great beauty come together in this instantly memorable and disturbing volume." — PUBLISHERS WEEKLY

About *Rational Numbers*

"Hix turns out keen metrics at once playful and soulful, suggesting that there may still be room for a philosophical modernist come lately." — HARVARD REVIEW

About *Perfect Hell*

"Hix has a dark, sexual and slightly sadistic sensibility coupled with an astonishing ability to fashion the haunting phrase and breathtaking image." —WASHINGTON POST BOOK WORLD

Also by H. L. Hix

Poetry

Surely As Birds Fly 2002

Rational Numbers 2000

Perfect Hell 1996

Translation

City of Ash (poetry by Eugenijus Ališanka) 2000

Philosophy/Criticism

Understanding William H. Gass 2002

Understanding W. S. Merwin 1997

Spirits Hovering Over the Ashes: Legacies of Postmodern Theory 1995

Morte d'Author: An Autopsy 1990

AS EASY AS LYING

Essays on Poetry

H. L. Hix

etruscan press

Etruscan Press
P.O. Box 9685
Silver Spring, MD 20916-9685
www.etruscanpress.org

Publisher's Cataloging-in-Publication
(Provided by Quality Books, Inc.)

Hix, H. L.
    As easy as lying : essays on peotry / H.L. Hix. --
1st ed.
    p. cm.
    ISBN 0-9718228-3-2

    1. Poetics. 2. Poetry.   I. Title.

PN1042.H59 2002   808.1
                           QBI02-200579

Contents

Acknowledgments   *vii*

First Books   *1*

Training for Poets   *7*

Covert Censorship   *23*

New Formalism among the Postmoderns   *28*

New Formalism at a Crossroads   *36*

Formal Experimentation and Poetic Discovery   *50*

On the (Ir)Regularity of Meter   *57*

Poetics   *65*

Abstraction's Command   *75*

Gently Omitting   *85*

Cold Baths   *88*

Toward a Prodigal Logic   *115*

Acknowledgments

Each of these essays has enjoyed a previous life—as a public presentation, in prior publication, or (in a few fortunate cases) both. I am grateful to the individuals responsible for inviting me to present these pieces and to the editors who first published them. Each has been altered since its initial appearance; for her help in this revision process, I am indebted to Debra Di Blasi.

Original publication venues for the essays were:
"Training for Poets": *The Iowa Review*.
"New Formalism among the Postmoderns": *Paintbrush*.
"New Formalism at a Crossroads": *Sparrow*.
"Formal Experimentation and Poetic Discovery": *Paintbrush*.
"On the (Ir)Regularity of Meter": *Interlitteraria*.
"Poetics": *Encyclopedia of Aesthetics*.
"Abstraction's Command": *Many Mountains Moving*.
"Gently Omitting": *Delmar*.
"Cold Baths": *Poetry International, Ploughshares, Harvard Review, Delmar*, and *New Letters*.

HAMLET:	Will you play upon this pipe?
GUILDENSTERN:	My lord, I cannot.
H:	I pray you.
G:	Believe me, I cannot.
H:	I do beseech you.
G:	I know no touch of it, my lord.
H:	It is as easy as lying.

AS EASY AS LYING

Essays on Poetry

First Books

The story of my first poetry book's publication holds little interest for anyone but me: poets, at least, already know it by heart, with names changed. Most poets either have lived it before or are living it now: I wrote and wrote for years; I collected hundreds of rejection slips, which I still keep in boxes, alphabetized; I revised and revised; I sent out queries, paid entry fees a decent broker could have parlayed by now into an impressive portfolio, made finalist often enough to break anyone's heart ("submission" strikes me as a ruthlessly accurate word); my book eventually won a contest and was published, but its parent manuscripts had been rejected so often that this scion's selection offered slender satisfaction, since I could attribute its success to nothing more than a reversal of fortune; the reviews were fine, but few; I had to badger the manager at my local Barnes & Noble to stock the book—may his soul, if soul he has, suffocate under a stack of discarded Danielle Steels—and badger him again to restock it after the first order sold out; few people bought it then; no one buys it now.

But so what? Poetry questions the preeminence of plot, the verity of the real, and even though its audience was tiny, my first poetry book's ambitions and its imagined consanguines still matter to me.

In her first book of prose, *Lyric Philosophy*, the poet Jan Zwicky avers that "the profoundly true utterance calls back to the world; calls us into being as auditors of that world. This is all that is meant by wisdom." I admire about that statement the perfect clarity provided by the very ambiguity of its first clause. Is the profoundly true utterance a part of the world that returns us (calls us back) to the world when we stray from the world? Or is it something outside the world that speaks (calls back) to the world from some other space, asking us to follow (at least with our eyes) beyond the world? Yes, to both possibilities.

Here duplicity counts as virtue, and I wanted such duplicitous wisdom to call back to the world from my first book, as I hear it call back in a book like Marie Howe's first, *The Good Thief*. From its opening poem, "Part of Eve's Discussion," Howe calls back to the world in just the way Zwicky urges. "It was like the moment," she begins, "when a bird decides not to eat from your hand, and flies, just before it flies." The simile calls us back to the world through the vivid tonality of its vehicles (the one just cited and the four that follow it). I do not say the vividness of their imagery, for it is not that through them I see something precise, but that through them I *feel* something precise. From her describing "it" as "very much like the moment, driving on bad ice, when it occurs to you your car could spin, just before it slowly begins to spin," I do not see it so much as I feel it. "It" does not designate my sight of the ice but my premonition-become-reality of the loss of traction.

Howe's withholding any explicit referent from the "it" in the poem calls back to the world in the other way also, from a space beyond. In testament to the force of metaphor, we the readers know from the title that the "it" in the poem refers to Eve's eating of the apple and consequent knowledge of good and evil, but we also know that "it" speaks of and from something beyond Eve, some unspecified part of the author's experience, and some (unspeakable) part of our own.

Having used "precise" to designate the Cartesian clarity-and-distinctness that serves Zwicky's duplicitous virtue of calling back to the world, I should say that precision also stands as a virtue in its own right, a virtue I sought, and another that Howe's book embodies, nowhere more perfectly for me than in her "How Many Times," where the narrator tries to "stop my father / from walking into my sister's room" but can't, because "This is the past / where everything is perfect already and nothing changes, // where the water glass falls to the bathroom floor / and bounces once before breaking." The unchanging events include "the small sound my sister makes, turning / over" and "the thump of the dog's tail / when he opens one eye" to watch the father "stumbling back to bed / still drunk, a little bewildered." In what posture does the dog lie in this poem? On its side, as the thumping of its tail on the floor reveals and its opening of only one eye seconds. With what material is the bathroom floor covered? Linoleum, as the glass's bouncing once before breaking reveals. Such precision elicits the hush to which Suzanne Noguere refers in her first book, the hush that "fell / upon the page as if light filtered through / trees to a forest floor." The same hush Wittgenstein tried to detail in the *Tractatus*: "What can be shown *cannot* be said."

No doubt my own statements are not as precise as I could wish. It may be that David Foster Wallace sums this up more succinctly in *Infinite Jest*: "Sometimes words that seem to express really evoke." The precision *with* which I speak here may not match the precision *of* which I speak, but only the latter allows a poem to give its reader insight, that combination of surprise and recognition that functions like stereoscopic vision to lend a poem depth beyond the flatness that, for me, the poems of Sharon Olds, say, or Gerald Stern sometimes display, in which the poem functions like the "Nudge, nudge, say no more, say no more" of the old Monty Python skit, as a code to members of a granfalloon, a name to validate an already familiar experience for one who has had it. I have never given birth, and, because it does not exceed ordinary precision or, therefore, offer surprised recognition, Olds's "The Moment the Two Worlds Meet," however it may speak to parents, especially to mothers, moves me no closer to that experience. In contrast, though I have never experienced or witnessed a father's sexual abuse of his child, Howe's extraordinarily precise poem brings me as far into that experience as words can.

I admire Marie Howe's first book, which illustrates some of the qualities I wanted my own first book to possess, but I might have celebrated other books in its stead, for the various strengths they model for me. Who would not want sentence structures as lush and rhythmic as those in Herbert Morris's *Peru* or the density of language and formal continuity in Richard Kenney's *The Evolution of the Flightless Bird*? Who would not envy Gjertrud Schnackenberg her historical sense and rhetorical elegance in *Portraits and Elegies* or Jared Carter his modest but diamond-hard clarity in *Work, for the Night Is Coming*?

If the successes I sought are several, the failures I fled are few, easy enough to enumerate: I wanted my first book of poetry to be neither too weak nor too strong. The flaw of weakness surely needs no explanation: so many nearly indistinguishable first books, by definition not worth naming, replete with what Donald Hall calls "McPoems," get published every year that I wanted not to increase their number, and I can only hope I have not. But my concern over the possibility of an opposite error does not arise from some neo-Aristotelian affirmation of a Golden Mean. (Would that I had had good reason while writing it to worry that my book might become too strong rather than too weak!)

A strong first book can pose a problem I name the "James Tate syndrome." I do not mean this as a cheap shot: I admire and follow Tate's work, I have some of his poems by heart, and I readily acknowledge him as *il miglior fabbro*. I only mean to observe that *The Lost Pilot* seems clearly the strongest and most distinctive of his books, not yet surpassed by any that have followed. In any case, like a termite infestation or colon cancer, this particular problem, of having made one's first book *too* strong, tends to reach an advanced stage before detection. A *weak* first book announces its failure immediately to any attentive and competent reader, but in the case of a *strong* first book, the James Tate syndrome reveals itself only over time, through a failure to surpass one's earliest work. Thus one must resist *before* its publication the threat of making one's first book too weak; but against the possibility of one's first book being too strong one must remain vigilant ever after.

A strong first book incurs, like any other manifestation of excellence, obligation. Virtues and vices do not simply cancel each other out. Good deeds cannot be stored up to exchange later for permission to perform pernicious ones, and Edgerrin James's current celerity will not suspend the salary cap later to let the Colts continue his contract for a few years after his knees are cabbage. Her otherwise beneficent life would make it *worse*, not better, if we learned posthumously that Mother Theresa had a bit of Bob Berdella in her. In poetry, the obligation is not merely self-reflectiveness, the ongoing critical evaluation of one's own work, achieved in the first stanza of Donald Justice's "Early Poems": "How fashionably sad those early poems are!" More important, a good first book obliges the *action* implied by Justice's last line: "Now the long silence. Now the beginning again." Self-reflection has value, but primarily as one step toward the ultimate obligation of improvement. Thus Pound's maxim, "The mastery of any art is the work of a lifetime," explains why, even if—even though—I failed to prevent my first book from being too weak, I must still guard against its being too strong.

If I could choose a model in this matter, it would be Elizabeth Bishop, who let "The Map" that starts her fine first book mercator her persistent preoccupations and her estimable talents, but without even hinting at the "First Death in Nova Scotia" and "Visits to St. Elizabeths" to follow.

I wanted my first book to be a prehistoric human body perfectly preserved in peat; the stenciled feathers and distorted skeleton of a saurian bird transformed to limestone; a gold-foil death mask that, repoussé merely to remember some minor regional baron, means Agamemnon now. I wanted my first book to illuminate, like a spelunker's lamp, a space older than our species but never seen before by human eyes; to speak in a wholly distinctive voice, a Linear B, its secrets ciphered for centuries; to attain that rarely occupied coign from which one sees more deeply into the world and farther beyond it simultaneously. I wanted my first book to be a feather tickling the clitoris of the world; the rhythmic ringing of steel on steel as a sledgehammer swung by a sweating coolie joined the country's coasts by rail; a goldfinch pinching thistle seed on a garden feeder in morning sunlight while the young boy watching it holds his breath.

If I failed to fulfill those ambitions in my first book, as of course I did, if the blood of my second is not as blue as those books I wanted for its brothers, if my third does not thrum a groundbass to the music of the spheres, surely my next book will bloom the little flower Blake calls the labor of ages. To live and write, one must *insist* on one's genius in spite of all evidence. Should my fourth book and my fifth fail like my first and second, I will, as they say in what passes for poetry where I come from, die trying.

Training for Poets

Critical discussion among poets suffers a void, especially notable now that American poetry pivots around M.F.A. programs, sites that tightly suture poetry production to pedagogy. So little has been written about *training* for the writing of poetry that the very idea hardly exists within contemporary poetry culture.

I know of no critical deficiency more glaring. Although most major general-interest periodicals ignore poetry and many literary journals run only palaverous reviews, a reader willing to seek out serious, discerning assessments of new collections can still find plenty; although much recent theorizing seems jejune, a writer seeking to satisfy her thirst for theory can find ample sustenance; even in these difficult financial times for university presses, a reader interested in practical criticism of contemporary poetry can mine from rich veins; and a practicing poet need not look far for advice about the act of poetic creation, the process of publication, or the task of teaching in a workshop context. But there awaits no equivalent wealth of work about what—when the workshop ends—continues to prepare one for poetic creation: the training of the poet. Nothing advises the poet on how to fulfill Roethke's admonition: "Make ready for your gifts. Prepare. Prepare."

Since the tempest in the teaching teacup rages, I should clarify that by "training" I do not refer here to pedagogy. Instead I mean to designate an ongoing process, as we would use the word to ask an athlete how her training was going, rather than a once-for-all process, as we would use the word to ask a doctor where he got his training. The training to which I refer resists the passive voice: grammar sanctions saying either that a doctor trained at Stanford or that he *received* his training there, but only sanctions saying of an Olympic champion that she trained in Boulder. Once-for-all training of the sort that leads to credentialing may have lasting benefits for poets, as it surely does for doctors: at the least, an earned M.D. from Johns Hopkins attests to having mastered a sizable body of basic knowledge about human physiology and nosology, and an M.F.A. from Iowa attests to the approbation of a group of established writers, themselves credentialed, whose judgment has currency among poetry writers and readers. Still, without the awareness that once-for-all training does not suffice, we would not laugh at the *New Yorker* cartoon that depicts a doctor in his office, degrees displayed prominently on the wall behind him, telling a visibly concerned couple: "No, I haven't performed the procedure myself, but I've seen it done successfully on *E.R.* and *Chicago Hope*." When I visit my HMO, I want to know that the doctor (or, more likely, nurse-practitioner) assigned me today earned respectable credentials at some point in the past, but also that she or he has stayed up to date since. In poetry, though, no body of literature debates practices parallel to those that keep a doctor current.

Discussion of the act or process of writing itself will not fill this void. Just as watching Pete Sampras's video on tennis technique will not help me turn pro if I am soft from years of exerting my service arm for nothing more vigorous than turning the pages of trade paperbacks and lifting mugs of lukewarm coffee, so learning from *The Triggering Town* that Richard Hugo wrote with a No. 2 pencil and crossed out "rapidly and violently" in preference to erasing may help my writing, but not much. Such knowledge of technique will not further my work if I am poetically "soft." I need training: I want to know what Richard Hugo did to prepare himself even to pick up a pencil. By analogy with the Kantian emphasis on being "even worthy of happiness," I must attempt to become even worthy of inspiration.

No doubt the absence of ongoing dialogue about training results in part from the lingering stereotype of the bohemian artist, whose vision derives from the posture of rebellion. But the deliquescence of the avant-garde reminds us of the other pole for the poet, opposite

8

bohemian disdain: discipline. *Any* posture—rebellious or not—without discipline decays almost immediately into postur*ing*: as a bunch like the Beats so plainly portrays. Reaffirmation of the importance of discipline to the practice of poetry will precede any constructive dialogue about training for poets.

I assume an analogy with athletic training but I also pursue a parallel to the case Iris Murdoch makes in *The Sovereignty of Good*—that "true vision occasions right conduct," with the substitution of voice rather than virtue as my aim. Thus, when Murdoch denies that freedom consists of "the sudden jumping of the isolated will in and out of an impersonal logical complex," asserting instead that it results from "the progressive attempt to see a particular object clearly," I want to apply her words to inspiration. Poetic inspiration occurs not upon the occasion of an unmotivated visit from a capricious muse but as a function of the poet's own progressive embodiment of an attitude toward language and the world. Murdoch aims her argument against existentialist ethics, and I aim mine in part against a common misconception popularized by confessionalism but often assumed about all poetry: the equation of a miserable life with good poetry. Kant points out, *contra* empiricism, that "though all our knowledge begins with experience, it does not follow that it all arises out of experience." Similarly, though the finest confessional poets lived tormented lives, it does not follow that their torment generated the great poetry. Millions of people have endured childhoods in the shadow of brutal father figures, but only one wrote "Daddy"; millions suffered manic depression before Prozac began mitigating its symptoms, yet only one wrote *The Dream Songs*. Plath and Berryman made great poetry beginning with their torment but not all out of it. They wrote great poetry because they were prepared to do so.

Murdoch's version of freedom and mine of inspiration share other similarities as well. Murdoch says: "I can only choose within the world I can see, in the moral sense of 'see' which implies that clear vision is a result of moral imagination and moral effort." Similarly, I argue, a poet can be inspired to write only what he has prepared himself to write, only what he can "see" because he has made the ongoing acts of readiness that give him the prerequisite clarity of vision.

Murdoch argues against choice as the fundamental moral action:

> . . . at crucial moments of choice most of the business of
> choosing is already over. . . . The exercise of our freedom is a
> small piecemeal business which goes on all the time and not a
> grandiose leaping about unimpeded at important moments.
> The moral life, on this view, is something that goes on con-
> tinually, not something that is switched off in between the
> occurrence of explicit moral choices. What happens in
> between such choices is indeed what is crucial.

Rather than exercising one's will in freedom while at the mall,
reaching as a result the conscious choice not to shoplift, one lives in
between trips to the mall in such a way that the need for that choice
never arises. The good person, on Murdoch's view, does not repeatedly
choose not to shoplift but instead trains her attention in such a way that
not shoplifting becomes a *fait accompli* before any occasion for choice
arises. "Our ability to act well 'when the time comes' depends partly,
perhaps largely, upon the quality of our habitual objects of attention,"
Murdoch says. "Freedom is not strictly the exercise of will, but rather
the experience of accurate vision. . . . By the time the moment of
choice has arrived the quality of attention has probably determined
the nature of the act." So in poetry. Jared Carter writes better poetry
than I do, not because at the moment of writing he consistently makes
better choices of words to include in his poems (though that effect
follows as a corollary), but because he has so highly elevated the
quality of the habitual objects of his attention.

Virtue in Murdoch's argument adopts perfection as an aim; voice in
mine, genius. Here the affinity between athletic training, Murdoch's
argument, and my claim coalesces: all assume a neo-Aristotelian view
about how to become what one is not. In all three cases, choice, the
spontaneous enacting of one possibility in preference to other possibilities, diminishes in importance before decision, the construction of a
deliberate fiction and its maintenance until it comes true. This fiction-
ality opens the space not of deceit or self-deception, but of mimesis. If
genius is not innate (and in so intertextual a realm as poetry, how could
it be?), it must be acquired by imitation. Become a flutist by acting as if
you were a flutist, not because you want to deceive others into thinking
you are already a flutist or because you suffer the delusion that you are a

flutist already, but because you can get to be a flutist only by doing what flutists do; and so for poets.

There's the rub. What *do* poets do? Beyond the obvious (they write poems), nobody's talking. What, exactly, do good poets or, better yet, great poets do to become so good? Go to the A.W.P. conference? I think a more interesting and more challenging answer begs formulation. The following fragments toward an answer will serve, I hope, as points of discussion. They presuppose a view of poetry as a synthetic activity, one that creates a unified work out of disparate components, so that training becomes what Hart Crane said the poet's concern must always be: "self-discipline toward a formal integration of experience."

I suggest therefore the following "curriculum" for a poet's training. As in any curriculum, breadth buttresses specialization, but imbalance is inevitable. The broader the base, the better, but no one can major in everything without failing, like the perennial student, by substituting the study itself for the objective it should serve. Each "major" also constitutes an important aspect of poetic practice, and by its being emphasized or downplayed can help establish a poet's voice, so I mention in each case a contemporary poet or poets whose work I see as emphasizing that aspect.

External

A poet's preparation begins with the extrapoetic, with "cross-training." Total immersion in poetry would drown anyone.

To falsify Dana Gioia's charge that "although American poetry sets out to talk about the world, it usually ends up talking about itself," poets will have to fulfill this imperative from George Oppen's daybook: "It is necessary to have some stance outside of Literature: it is necessary to be disconnected with literature." Oppen may have had in mind a specifically political stance, but I construe "stance" more broadly. Each poet must establish her stance, define her disconnection, as she sees fit, whether through political engagement, study of another field, employment in a capacity unrelated to poetry, or some other way.

This category does not parallel those that follow. In many cases, adoption of "a stance outside of Literature" happens by necessity (in employment, for instance) or without conscious decision (as when someone comes to poetry through a formative experience such as involvement in a war). Also, training in one of the other categories may itself produce or relate to one's "stance outside of Literature." Still, the caveat that one must bring to poetry something other than poetry demands statement, and acquiring or developing that stance will constitute an important part of any poet's training. Study physics. Tend bar. Become a doctor or engineer. Serve in the Peace Corps. Hike the Appalachian Trail. Besides the familiar bank clerks, insurance executives, and doctors from the modernist canon, I know, or know of, poets whose "stance outside of Literature" derives from current or former careers as musicians, schoolteachers, plumbers, farmers, business executives, and housecleaners, as well as poets who teach creative writing for a living but who create a stance from active engagement in mountaineering, horse training, political activism, and so on.

Again, this category does not parallel those that follow, so perhaps any good poet (other than a Stevens, whose every poem seems an *ars poetica*) would serve as an example of emphasis on the "external," but in a poetry world still beholden to the old New Critics and still most comfortable accepting as "poetic" the concerns of white males, poets such as Adrienne Rich and Marilyn Nelson stand out as poets whose work foregrounds what I am calling the "external." Without neglecting other poetic concerns (the sound of the language, the relation to poetic tradition, and so on), each subordinates those concerns to the service of the extrapoetic "content" of the poems: in Rich, validation of the experiences and the rights of women in general and lesbians in particular, and in Nelson, exploration of the experience of being an African-American woman. When emphasis on the external fails (as so often in devotional poetry, for example), poetry becomes merely didactic; when it succeeds (as so often in Rich and Nelson), it reorients a reader toward some neglected portion of his own experience or alerts the reader to ways in which another person's experience differs from his own, fulfilling the most catholic version of the ideal implicit in Simone de Beauvoir's assertion that "There is a whole region of human experience which the male deliberately chooses to ignore because he fails to *think* it: this experience woman *lives*."

Verbal

In addition to having something besides poetry to write poems about, a poet needs the verbal facility to write them well. Indeed, the two capacities cannot be separated. In Nietzsche's formulation: "We always express our thoughts with the words that lie to hand. Or, to express my whole suspicion: we have at any moment only the thought for which we have to hand the words." No one will need convincing on this point: from the monthly installment of "Increase Your Word Power" in *Reader's Digest* to ads in business magazines promising career success through expansion of vocabulary, we see repeated acknowledgment throughout society of the general importance of verbal skills. Nor, within the particular practice of poetry, does anyone construe as accidental the correlation between Shakespeare's rich vocabulary and the richness of his plays.

Most poets enjoy unusual verbal fluency already, or they would not have entertained the ambition of becoming a poet, and much of the method for further enrichment is self-evident: read a lot and write a lot. Still, two practices seem especially important to verbal training. First is the study of languages other than English (or other than one's native tongue). Study of languages closely related to English, like the classical and Romance languages, underscores grammatical and etymological understanding of English. In languages more distantly related to English, the underscoring of grammatical understanding occurs through contrast, and a glimpse at the absence of precise correlatives for words and locutions from another language heightens sensitivity to nuance in English. Until the middle of this century, most of the now-canonical poets in the Anglo-American tradition (those "English poets who grew up on Greek") learned at least Latin in youth, and most of the contemporary poets I know speak or read at least one other language.

The second practice is simple enlargement of English vocabulary. Dip into the dictionary daily. Note unfamiliar words as you read, and prepare small cards for each: write the new word on one side of the card, and on the other side write its definitions along with an example sentence, preferably the one in which you first saw the word. Periodic review helps a word stay in mind until either another encounter with it or some occasion for its use plants it firmly in mind. Whatever the method, enlarging vocabulary serves a poet's development: only from a broad palette can one hope to produce the precise shades of meaning poetry demands.

So-called language poetry got its name from emphasizing this aspect of poetry, but any work written on the basis of an attempt to liberate the generative powers of language by diminishing the intentional and expressive role of the author (in favor of the language's own "expression" of "intention") would exemplify this characteristic. Rule-bound texts such as John Cage's mesostics feature the verbal over the other aspects of poetry, as do "intertextual" works such as Rosmarie Waldrop's *The Reproduction of Profiles*. Heather McHugh and S. X. Rosenstock, whose work abounds in puns and wordplay, demonstrate a different way of featuring language above other aspects of poetry. Such poetry fails when its language becomes merely a private language and functions, like role-playing games, to draw the imagination farther and farther into an isolated world. It succeeds when it fulfills Gadamer's directive that "the proper function of the poet is a shared saying, a saying that possesses absolute reality simply by virtue of its being said," and therefore embodies Wittgenstein's maxim that "What looks as if it *had* to exist, is part of the language"; when, in other words, it reveals things that not only *do* exist but *must* exist.

Musical

Certainly music bears a relation to poetry different from that of words, though a no less integral one. The intensity of poetic language cannot be separated from its musicality, and many musical elements—rhythm, harmony, tone, melody, and so on—cross over either literally or metaphorically into poetry.

But isn't it music*ality*, one might ask, that matters in poetry, rather than music *per se*? Besides, since society surrounds us with music in grocery stores and waiting rooms, at the movies and on the bus, in our cars and in our homes, why would *a* poet need special musical training? Of course a poet does need musicality to compose in a voice as canorous as Bogan or Bishop, Hopkins or Hecht, and one can acquire musicality by listening to language: recite enough Keats, and soon your sentences, too, will sing. Still, music remains the root of musicality, and training in the former should enhance the latter. Dickinson made hay out of humming old hymns, but imagine the range a broader repertoire could have handed her. As for our being deluged with music, we are, but in the role of passive receptors and to such a degree that we learn to shut the music out. Most of us very seldom function as *active* listeners to or, better, as *makers of* music, and only when we assume those roles can we indenture music into our service as poets.

Bruce Bond, Donald Justice, and Jan Zwicky, who have extensive professional training in music and who sometimes write poems on the subject of music, foreground musicality, but so do Eric Pankey's recent poems, the lush and melodic cadences of which draw on the riches of music as their greatest resource. Poetry that emphasizes musicality fails when it slips into Swinburnian singsong divorced from sense but succeeds when the emotive power of absolute music fills the language of the poem "up to the brim, and even above the brim."

Traditional

"I am a traditionalist," James Wright says, "and I think that whatever we have in our lives that matters has to do with our discovering our true relation to the past." One need not share Wright's traditionalism, though, to recognize the importance of thorough knowledge of the tradition within which one writes. Even the most virulent antitraditionalist needs a deep awareness of tradition. Adorno says: "One must have tradition in oneself, to hate it properly"—or, more mildly yet purposefully stated, to resist it effectively.

In advocating knowledge of tradition—the discovery, in Wright's words, of one's true relation to the past—I do not assume a narrow view of "the tradition." One important development for poetry in the last thirty years has been recognition that the history of poetry as the New Critics saw it, the history being narrated in classrooms as the Creative Writing M.F.A. established itself, was *a* history of poetry, and that even though immersion in that tradition mattered, immersion in that tradition *alone* was highly confining. We must acknowledge and understand not only the alternative traditions created all along by politically underserved groups such as women and ethnic minorities but also the alternative traditions as defined formally or by other criteria. Discovering the richest possible tradition for oneself, without blindly accepting a narrow or impoverished one handed down, becomes the mandate.

Memorize poems. Memorize many. One a week for twenty years is not too much. The concerns some parents and religious fundamentalists express about the pervasiveness of "adult themes" in movies, radio, television, and other media can be easily exaggerated but they have a basis in fact: filling the mind of a child (or an adult) with violence and pornography will not by itself cause that child to commit violent or perverse acts but it certainly would combine with any other influences to support inclinations in that direction. Similarly, I believe, memorizing a large body of fine poetry will not cause one to become an excellent poet but will combine with any other training practices to support that ambition.

Any "neo-" movement defines itself by its relation to the past, so "New Formalism" stands as the most visible current expression of tradition as the central poetic element. Dana Gioia, for example, differentiates his work from others in part by adopting (explicitly in his criticism and implicitly in his poetry) previously unfashionable predecessors such as Kees and Longfellow as his ancestors. A different approach that still foregrounds tradition can be found in Susan Wheeler's work, with its more ironic method of borrowing. Traditionalist poetry fails when it merely follows models, repeating what preceded it, and succeeds when it restores to the repertoire of poetry some neglected power stored in form.

Physical

Here the familiar adage, *"mens sana in corpore sano,"* holds as always. Mental function cannot be severed from somatic: the effects on mental function of chemical alterations and circulatory problems have been amply documented, and anyone can verify from personal experience how much more difficult concentration becomes during a bad cold or other illness, and how much longer and more vigorously one can work during periods of good health. Even in that most paradigmatically cerebral sport, chess, the Soviet training system that dominated the world for years included ambitious physical exercise programs. Karpov looked clumsy on the tennis courts, but he spent a lot of time there and always looked good at the chessboard afterward.

Because this facet of training seems *prima facie* farthest removed from the stereotyped poet in the garret, and because the history of great poetry brims with examples of poor physical specimens, from tubercular Keats to bingeing Berryman, I should insert here a disclaimer that applies to all the types of training in this essay. I do not assert that the degree of one's physical fitness bears some direct correlation with excellence in poetry: Jackie Joyner-Kersee can't trade her gold medals for Rita Dove's Pulitzer. I do allege that, *all else being equal*, physical fitness furthers the work of poetry by enhancing relevant qualities such as concentration and endurance. Excellence in any one area of training will not by itself translate into excellence in poetry; discipline in all the areas, however, will accrue to the benefit of anyone's poetry.

So run or ride a mountain bike or take up basketball. Exercise need not stand alone in a physical training regimen for a poet, though, since fitness does not stand alone as a physical concern. Poetry is written by bodies and about bodies, so any practice that promotes coenesthesis will contribute, from yoga or T'ai Chi to meditation or even—all work and no play makes a dull poet—sex.

Molly Peacock and Sharon Olds foreground the physical in their poetry, Peacock often and Olds almost always. One could not read the first section of Peacock's *Original Love*, for instance, without being reminded that the voice, whatever its relation to the mind, always and necessarily speaks most immediately from the body. Preoccupation with the physical succeeds when it heightens self-awareness, helping the poet and reader place themselves in the world more precisely; it fails when it falls into fascination, when (replicating, in a different province, the failure of language poetry) it pulls the imagination into a privacy severed from reciprocity with the world (the body/bodies) outside the body.

17

Chthonic

In addition to awareness of one's own body, awareness of the other bodies around us (animal, vegetable, and mineral) serves the poet, as Thoreau indicates with his rhetorical questions: "Shall I not have intelligence with the earth? Am I not partly leaves and vegetable mould myself?" As population continues to migrate toward cities, and as culture becomes more and more exclusively produced in urban settings, this aspect of an individual poet's training increases in importance. As the proportion of our perceptual energies devoted to storefront and monitor and billboard rises, so do we more closely resemble the urban child who does not know that hamburgers come from cows. Even a city dweller needs to retain some awareness of those aspects of experience not specific to the city.

The pull toward gardening as a means of maintaining primal intimacy with the earth must be strong, since gardening remains the most popular pastime in the world, and since its beneficial effects on at-risk children, for instance, seem clear. But gardening hardly exhausts the options for chthonic connection: through their recent anthology, Joseph Duemer and Jim Simmerman have demonstrated how powerfully dogs can draw out one's reciprocity with the earth; Don Welch raises pigeons; W. S. Merwin cultivates plants native to his current home state.

Pattiann Rogers and Mary Oliver heavily emphasize the chthonic in their poetry. In Oliver's *American Primitive*, for example, nearly every poem takes as its subject some natural phenomenon ("Lightning," "First Snow," "Spring"), some plant or animal ("Mushrooms," "Moles," "Egrets"), or some human activity in a natural setting ("Tasting the Wild Grapes," "Crossing the Swamp"). Such poetry succeeds when it meets the Augustinian ideal, "He lives in justice and sanctity who is an unprejudiced assessor of the intrinsic value of things," and fails when it romanticizes nature. Romanticizing does two things wrong at once: it engages in the exploitation Jan Zwicky says "occurs when a thing . . . is used in the absence of a perception of what it is," and it flows from self-deception, specifically the denial of one's own complicated and ambiguous relation with the earth.

Cultural

At the pole opposite the chthonic lies the cultural, the realm of specifically human construction, no less essential a part of any poet's
awareness. Poetry and music are obviously cultural products, but I
have made the "traditional" and "musical" into their own categories
because of the peculiarly close relation each has to the practice of a
poet, leaving "cultural" to function here as a catchall for other forms
of human production.

I argued in *Spirits Hovering Over the Ashes* that the twentieth century
has witnessed a sea change in the most pervasive view of culture, from a
diachronic perspective in which one defined oneself temporally, by
relation to one's predecessors, to a synchronic perspective in which one
defines oneself by relation to one's contemporaries. I argued there for a
balance between the two views, neither of which stands complete in
itself and each of which depends for its efficacy on the presence of the
other. I suggest here that within the specific realm of poetry the same
need for balance holds. A poet must constantly increase her knowledge
of and sensitivity to the cultural products of the past and also to the
breadth of contemporary cultural products. Read history and art history.
Travel. Read beyond the body of mostly Euro-American, white, male
writers on whose work most of us were fed in our formal education. Read
more deeply into that body of writers. Surround yourself with artists or
physicists instead of other poets.

Poets such as Gjertrud Schnackenberg and Richard Howard typify
an emphasis on the diachronic cultural, responding to earlier cultural
artifacts; poets such as Naomi Shihab Nye and David Mura typify an
emphasis on the synchronic cultural, drawing out the importance of
cultural context and the breadth of available culture beyond the Euro-
American. Poetry that emphasizes the diachronic cultural succeeds
when it illuminates its contemporary concerns by establishing their
timelessness through connection with earlier culture, and fails when it
falls into nostalgia or mere erudition. Poetry that emphasizes the synchronic cultural succeeds when it reveals the universality of private,
"tribal" concerns, when in other words it makes possible a new cultural

awareness to any party willing to engage it, and fails when it speaks only to those already attuned to its cultural domain.

Communal

Writing poetry occurs not as an exclusively solitary occupation but within various communities, including at least one built around poetry and at least one other that does not acknowledge the poetry being written and read within it. Part of a poet's training consists in the fulfillment of his obligations to the community/communities within which he writes.

Fulfillment of one's obligation to the poetry community can occur in various ways. Reviewing for a journal or teaching in an M.F.A. program would accomplish this end, as would editing and some forms of criticism. Fulfillment of one's obligation to the broader community, the one that does not recognize or acknowledge the poetry being written within it, may be more difficult because of the scope of the problem. As Charles Bernstein so succinctly formulated it: "What is to be regretted is not the lack of mass audience for any particular poet but the lack of poetic thinking as an activated potential for all people." Write criticism aimed at a general-interest audience rather than at an audience of those previously engaged in reading poetry, or go into the schools. Other enterprises such as anthologizing might serve the same end: Naomi Nye's anthology work for children offers a good example. Those poets who have founded presses (New Directions, Ecco, Copper Canyon, Story Line, and so on) provide the most dramatic example of service to both communities simultaneously and substantially.

A vivid example of a body of work in which community stands as the central element is that of Carolyn Forché, not only in her own poetry but also in her translation and anthologizing. "Communal" poetry succeeds when it awakens readers to the experiences of other community members or generates in the reader a recognition of her membership in communities with which she had not previously identified, and so furthers the solidarity of humans; it fails when it makes mere melodrama of the circumstances and lives it depicts.

Conceptual

Identifying the "conceptual" as a training component demonstrates again how little the categories can be separated. After all, elements such as musicality might well be considered conceptual. Still, a realm exists, however much it may overlap with the preceding domains, that Vilhelm Ekelund's words encapsulate: "Everything beautiful wants to tell you something. Everything beautiful wants to become thought."

Maintain a daybook or journal. The list is long of poets whose extensive journals underwrote their poems: George Oppen, Theodore Roethke, Sylvia Plath, and others. Even correspondence on a high level can advance this aim, as attested by the letters of Keats, Williams, Olson/Creeley, and others. To that list one might add criticism as well, particularly criticism with a theoretical rather than a practical bent.

Richard Kenney, Jorie Graham, and Robert Bringhurst emphasize the conceptual. Kenney's use of scientific terminology and ideas, Graham's particular manner of appropriating the cultural (which seems to me to fit better here than into the "cultural" category above), and Bringhurst's uses of the pre-Socratics and Eastern thought all pursue a "mystical rationality" not unlike that toward which some philosophers strive. Poetry that foregrounds the conceptual succeeds when it accomplishes the Kantian aim of synthetic *a priori* knowledge and fails when it becomes idle speculation, the Wittgensteinian "wheel that can be turned though nothing else moves with it" and which therefore "is not part of the mechanism."

Discipline not balanced by spontaneity and play and eccentricity and idleness produces anorexics and flagellants, not poets. I have exaggerated the emphasis on discipline in this essay because both the poetry community and the broader culture suffer from an aspect blindness in regard to poetry, a repression of the role of discipline. Religion suffers when either its practitioners or its opponents diminish the role discipline plays in it (when they treat it, for example, as primarily a social outlet or a self-help strategy), and so does poetry. This essay has been imbalanced *toward* discipline because prevailing views of poetry are imbalanced *away from* it, and a poetic practice (or any other life) with too *little* discipline sacrifices as much satisfaction as does a poetic practice with too much.

Nietzsche answers his own question "What is genius?" with two conditions: "To will an exalted end *and* the means to it." The first condition every aspiring poet fulfills, but the second has been my concern here. To will the means to the exalted end of writing fine poetry, a poet must enact the Keatsian imperative to "inspect the lyre, and weigh the stress / Of every chord, and see what may be gain'd / By ear industrious, and attention meet." Training that attends to the elements enumerated above will serve any poet, fostering in her or him a set of skills and awarenesses that can catalyze the writing process, and embodying a set of core values—consistency, self-discipline, and so on—that, though seldom dramatized as part of the image of the poet in our society, regularly present themselves in the character and practices of the great poets who preceded us.

Covert Censorship

No one opposes all censorship, or censorship *per se*. I may disagree with Tipper Gore about whether to ban the lyrics of Snoop Dogg's songs, but I have to agree with her that our government, and indeed any government, can and should censor certain forms of speech. For instance, the law rightly damns the illicit glossal licenses we name slander and libel. I should be prevented from publishing in the local newspaper an article alleging a colleague's active engagement in a torrid affair with a seventeen-year-old freshman student, when I know both the falsity of the allegation and our employer's prohibition against that type of teacher-student relationship. Similarly, other forms of verbal expression (in addition to old standards like crying "Fire!" in a crowded theater) ought to be denied me. I should be prevented from making threatening phone calls to my neighbors; I should not be allowed to distribute to schoolchildren leaflets advertising my pornographic home videos; and so on.

Words can be weapons, and danger limits their legitimate use. The broad question, then, is not whether there should be censorship, but what should be censored, by whom, and under what conditions. Not whether any censorship at all is good, but what censorship is good and what censorship is bad.

Not that I will answer that broad question. My nihilism leads me to suspect that no satisfactory answer exists, and in any case *I* don't have one. I formulate the question to draw attention to its complexity: yes or no will not answer a question that ranges over an infinite variety of works and circumstances, each unique. Inability to provide an adequate answer to the question does not, however, relieve one of the responsibility to ask it and to explore it.

A law that tries by appeal to "community standards" to identify the conditions under which censorship is appropriate only names the problem but does not solve it. Not only are community standards usually difficult to identify, seldom universal, and always changing, but—more important—discourse, including the discourse of the arts, acts as a primary agent of change in community standards. Defining good censorship by community standards assumes tacitly (and falsely) that maintenance of the status quo ought to be a universal community standard. The paradox that complicates the issue of censorship is that community standards can be created only by destroying other community standards. Artists become artists in part through subverting community standards: like Shelley's west wind, we are both the destroyers and the preservers of community standards.

At our best, we are revolutionaries. Not necessarily political revolutionaries; most of us most of the time are (and ought to be) content to leave the job of overthrowing the government to members of the Michigan Militia. More often, we act as metaphysical revolutionaries, holding up to the status quo a competing vision of the true and beautiful and good. In Donald Barthelme's words: "It's our good fortune to be able to imagine alternative realities, other possibilities. We can quarrel with the world, constructively."

In response to a competing vision of the world, murder is the sincerest form of flattery. The murder of an artist constitutes a public acknowledgment by the murderer that the artist's vision betters his own. Artist and martyr are twin progeny of different parents, and the late Ayatollah Khomeini was a more influential critic than Helen Vendler.

Do not mistake my claim. Sometimes praise of the work injures the artist; I oppose aggression; and the Ayatollah was an ass. I only mean that we more often notice and resist censorship that aims to punish artists than censorship that aims to diminish art. I mean that we see the threat Jesse Helms poses and we resist it, though Barnes & Noble censors more effectively.

I mean that censorship is more complex than clear-cut. I mean that you and I are complicit. I mean that the A.W.P. censors no less effectively than does the Alabama Board of Education. Our ambition cannot be to eliminate censorship altogether, only to censor more accurately, to use better judgment in censoring.

The biggest censorship problem art itself faces is not that artists are being prevented from presenting their competing visions of the world (though, I reiterate, I do not diminish the magnitude of that problem for the artists); art itself suffers more from our failure to persuade the world that those competing visions pose a threat. The biggest problem for *artists* is that so many are dying for their art; the biggest problem for *art itself* is that so few are dying.

Because doing so stimulates capital flow, media capitalism makes the ability to interest large numbers of people, simultaneously and briefly, definitive of newsworthiness and of aesthetic value. In other words, it propagates monoculture. Advocates of multiculturalism waste their time opposing the Bob Packwoods and outshouting the Marge Schotts if they then return home to *E.R.* and Tom Brokaw: nothing more effectively erases multiplicity of culture than TV. Similarly, advocates of art get fixated on flash points and forget the forest fire.

Market forces discourage deep ideas and new ideas. Shallow ideas increase the consumer base: no unusual intelligence is required to read *People* magazine and no advanced education to understand the latest Danielle Steel novel, so the potential audience vastly exceeds that of more taxing products such as *The Georgia Review* and Linda Gregerson's poems. Shallow ideas even shorten shelf life: shallow reading is fast reading, so you must read (and therefore buy) more pages to occupy the same amount of time. Not only must one allot more time to read the words on the page when they convey new ideas or deep ideas, but the ideas themselves demand "time out" to think. Thinking about what you read is one thing Simon & Schuster and Waldenbooks do not want you to do. If you chew each mouthful thirty times, you will lose weight because you will consume less at each meal, and if you think about what you read you will consume fewer books from B. Dalton.

Artists cannot but state a minority opinion. The artist fits Nietzsche's definition of a nihilist: one who "judges of the world as it is that it ought not to be, and of the world as it ought to be that it does not exist." The artist, at least in her successful moments, sees the world accurately and (therefore) posits an alternative.

Albert Camus distinguishes thus between rebellion and revolution: "Rebellion is, by nature, limited in scope. It is no more than an incoherent pronouncement. Revolution, on the contrary, originates in the realm of ideas. Specifically, it is the injection of ideas into historical experience. . . . A revolution is an attempt to shape actions to ideas, to fit the world into a theoretic frame." Artists at their best are not rebels but revolutionaries. Art cannot afford to subscribe fully to community standards. It always proposes a re-vision of the community, a reconstruction of the theoretic frame into which we fit ourselves.

Overt censors like Helms believe that their censorship stamps out rebellion, and most defenders of art have fallen for that assumption because it permits a defense based on the assertion that art does not threaten: rebels are less dangerous than they seem; artists are pests, but if you ignore them you will suffer no lasting harm. But such defenses mistakenly denigrate art. Artists are more dangerous than Jesse Helms even in his wildest paranoid and jingoistic fantasies can imagine, because at our best we are revolutionaries rather than rebels.

Our work threatens Helms's beliefs more than he knows, and his censorship threatens our work not at all. (Our work, mind you. He does threaten us: overt censors are killers. But to our work, they are publicists. I, who despised literature in high school, would never have read *Catcher in the Rye* had it not been prohibited. Without censorship, Mapplethorpe and Salman Rushdie might have faded as fast as irises, but now our grandchildren will view and read their work.) For our work we should fear not overt censors but covert censors: Waldenbooks, Time Warner, ourselves. Not to die but to be co-opted is the artist's worst fate: to become part of the status quo and therefore able only to rebel but not to revolt.

To put all this in one last frame, I borrow Václav Havel's suggestion from "The Power of the Powerless" that the presence and the effectiveness of covert censorship implies an imperative for those of us with ambitions as artists. In that 1978 essay, Havel argues that what he calls the "post-totalitarian" state, referring to the Soviet bloc at that time, resembles market capitalism more than it differs from it: "The hierarchy of values existing in the developed countries of the West has, in essence, appeared in our society," but this creates "a yawning abyss: while life, in its essence, moves toward plurality, diversity, independent self-constitution, and self-organization, in short, toward the fulfillment of its own freedom, the post-totalitarian system demands conformity, uniformity, and discipline." Only by dissent, by revolution rather than rebellion, can one choose what Havel calls "life" over what he calls "the system."

Havel creates a fictive greengrocer who one day stops putting the mandatory slogans in his shop window, who "rejects the ritual and breaks the rules of the game." In so doing, the greengrocer "has not committed a simple, individual offense, isolated in its own unique-ness, but something incomparably more serious. By breaking the rules of the game, he has disrupted the game as such. He has exposed it as a mere game."

We must adapt the greengrocer's integrity in response to the game of monoculture. As with Havel's greengrocer, the acts need not be monumental to be effective. I once worked with a group of friends to produce a journal that was distributed free. Most of us make a practice of frequenting independent booksellers and reading small-press books. A Canadian poet I know turned down offers of publication for her recent book in favor of hand-sewing her own signatures. And always there remains our work itself: unpredictable, out of fashion, relent-less—or dead.

On a trip to the former Soviet Union in 1994, I learned that poetry had dwindled in importance upon liberation. When overt censorship stopped threatening their lives, poets faced a different challenge: covert censorship threatened the life of their work. That challenge, covert cen-sorship, is the one artists face most often, and only by our small but endlessly iterated acts of dissent can we resist the marasmus of mono-culture.

New Formalism among the Postmoderns

New Formalism and postmodernism might seem at first glance antithetical, and since "postmodernism," as the older and more catholic term, enjoys (or suffers) wider use in academia and in popular culture, New Formalists have been tempted at times to individuate New Formalism by opposing it to postmodernism, as Kevin Walzer does in his monograph about New Formalism, *The Ghost of Tradition*. But assume instead that, as New Formalism taps a richer vein than postmoderns such as Perloff opine, so postmodernism holds more ore than New Formalists such as Walzer acknowledge: then the antithesis dissipates, freeing New Formalism to learn from its elder.

Toward that more salubrious relationship between New Formalism and postmodernism, I offer here, first, three observations about postmodernism, each calculated to paint it, in its poetic and theoretical manifestations, as at least *motivated*. Not sound or adequate or true, none of which I would aver, but motivated, and therefore worthy of more serious attention than the dismissal as idle and irresponsible that I have heard from more than one New Formalist. After the three observations about postmodernism, I briefly note three misconceptions about the relationship between postmodernism and New Formalism, observing that, however tempting the misconceptions might be for a proponent of New Formalism, each results from oversimplification, specifically from a false dilemma. I intend each of these statements (of the three observations and the three misconceptions) to be descriptive, hoping the essay will be informative, but to each I will add a prescriptive assertion, hoping to make this essay useful to practicing poets.

OBSERVATION 1: Postmodernism Responds to Technological Change

One of the forces driving postmodernism is the speed and magnitude of technological change in this century, especially in the technology of "information processing." The issue merits attention because technological developments change us and our poetry, and historical perspective helps because rhyme and meter, two of the three components typically said to define New Formalism, themselves function as information-processing "technologies" or techniques.

New information-processing technologies change human individuals and groups. By the 1920s, A. R. Luria had demonstrated conclusively that the information-processing technology we call writing changes the neurophysiology of human individuals: learning to read and write alters the structure of neural connections in the brain. Socrates had argued for a related conclusion in Plato's *Phaedrus*, contending (with some warrant) that writing destroys the memory. History displays vividly the impact of new information-processing technologies on social groups. The two greatest cultural flowerings in Western history correlate with the two most significant advances in information-processing technology before this century: Classical Greece, with its gifts of philosophy, democracy, the literary mode we call tragedy, and unrivaled advances in art and architecture, followed hard on the heels of the Greek adoption of the Phoenician alphabet in approximately 730 b.c., and the European Renaissance flowered in season with Gutenberg's invention of the printing press in the mid-1400s.

Postmodernism, in its theoretical and poetic manifestations, attempts to grapple with the meaning of a recent set of nearly simultaneous developments in information-processing media (radio, television, and film; telephones and faxes; computers) that together constitute the most dramatic information revolution in human history. In doing so, postmodernism suggests an avenue of thought that might prove beneficial to New Formalism's self-understanding and apologetics. The features New Formalism calls form, sonic patterns of rhyme and regular meter, originated (like poetry itself) in oral cultures, that is, among people separated from us not only by a few centuries but by several technology-related alterations to our identity. A deeper understanding of the mnemonic (and other) purposes that rhyme and meter served in their original contexts would help explain why these formal techniques have persisted through drastic changes in information technology and would enrich the basis for New Formalism's sense of their contemporary function and importance by explaining their perduring vitality.

Observation 2: Postmodernism Responds to Cultural Change

Postmodernism alters the relative valuation of space and time. A modernist such as T. S. Eliot values time more highly. He thinks meaning springs from diachrony and attributes the profundity of great poems to their having internalized the prior history of great poems. Eliot thinks that diachrony governs the act of creation (obliging the poet to "develop or procure the consciousness of the past") and also governs the reception of the work (which can be valued only by setting the artist "for contrast and comparison, among the dead," and by judging the artist according to "the standards of the past").

In contrast, postmoderns more highly value space, a view most succinctly formulated in that precocious postmodernist, Saussure, who sees meaning as constituted exclusively by synchrony, so that one who wishes to understand linguistic meaning "must discard all knowledge of everything that produced it and ignore diachrony. He can enter into the mind of speakers only by completely suppressing the past. The intervention of history can only falsify his judgment."

In other words, modernists view the constitutive other (the external source of their identity and of the meaning of their work, that which is/was what they are) as distributed across time, but postmodernists, because they see difference as the source of meaning, see the constitutive other as distributed across space, viewing their identities as constructed by their difference from other contemporaries rather than by continuity with their antecedents.

A New Formalist might find in this idea a fruitful way of thinking about what makes New Formalism *new*. Why is Mary Jo Salter a New Formalist, but not Elizabeth Bishop? Why is David Mason a New Formalist, but not Robert Frost? The obvious answer, that Salter and Mason are younger (and still living), makes "New Formalist" merely a historical, not an aesthetic, category, *unless* postmodern theory is right that identity and meaning arise through the place something occupies in a synchronic system, specifically through its difference from other items in the system. Then the use of traditional rhyme and meter by someone of Mary Jo Salter's age may mean something significantly different from what it meant for someone of Elizabeth Bishop's generation, and the use of traditional narrative techniques by someone of David Mason's age may mean something significantly different from what it meant for Frost. No longer *accidental* to aesthetic identity, age becomes essential, and the use of similar formal techniques in different social and historical contexts may have different aesthetic effects and value.

OBSERVATION 3: Postmodernism Resists What It Calls "Totalization"

Jean-François Lyotard argues that what he calls "the postmodern condition" arises from a loss of grand narratives. Technological and cultural changes have led to the translation of knowledge "into quantities of information" and consequently to "a thorough exteriorization of knowledge with respect to the 'knower'" (a grade-schooler seeking information today will go not to a knowledgeable person but to the Internet) and to "the mercantilization of knowledge" (for-profit higher education corporations are hot stocks these days). These changes might lead to either of two states of affairs: 1) a system in which access to knowledge becomes highly centralized, controlled by only a few very powerful individuals, with the result Lyotard calls "terror," a sharp increase in the efficiency of the system, achieved by expanding the ability of some individuals to eliminate others from participation in the system; or 2) a system in which consensus becomes "an outmoded and suspect value," allowing players to determine the rules of the game locally, with the result Lyotard calls "justice."

Lyotard's observation frames an alternative explanation for the waxing interest in narrative in poetry. One standard explanation runs like this. Prose (especially the novel) took over narrative from poetry. Modernism made a virtue of this necessity, insisting as a matter of principle on the exclusion of plot from poetry. Mass media (TV and film) confirmed the separation and reduced poets in creative writing departments to defending the borders of the reservation. New Formalists rebelled, recapturing this lost tradition.

But viewed through Lyotard's lens, historical variations in the legitimacy of narrative in poetry need not be seen as exclusively (or primarily) literary in their causes and effects. New Formalism ceases to be a strictly literary movement of interest primarily to those actively engaged with contemporary poetry. Not only can its causation be seen in a broader context, as something having to do with more than literature, but so can its effects. New Formalism can be seen as furthering Lyotard's ideal of justice by helping to "de-totalize" whom society authorizes to tell what stories, since it reinvigorates the local authority to access and implement the "information technologies" resident in poetry, thus furthering Lyotard's ambition for the "free access" to memory/data that transforms language games into "games of perfect information at any given moment," helping to diminish terror and to further justice.

MISCONCEPTION 1: New Formalists Use Form; Postmodernists Do Not

Certainly such a statement overgeneralizes, since a "postmodern" book such as Ron Silliman's *What* employs rhyme throughout, and a "New Formalist" book like Dana Gioia's *The Gods of Winter* includes free-verse poems. More importantly, though, the view that New Formalists use form and postmodernists do not could hold only if "form" meant *exclusively* "traditional forms" such as the sonnet, the villanelle, and blank verse. But why should it count as form when Molly Peacock writes a sonnet, but not when Lyn Hejinian writes *My Life* with a section for each of her 45 years and 45 sentences per section? No one benefits from construing form so narrowly.

The misconception could be limited to the contention that New Formalists embrace meter and postmodernists reject it. Even that assertion is misleading at best, implying that meter is something a particular stretch of language either possesses or does not possess. Such an absolute distinction cannot hold. Dana Gioia points out that "The Red Wheelbarrow," that apparently unmetered free-verse poem, actually scans as blank verse, and Timothy Steele shows that iambic pentameter admits of a wide range of variation. If meter means *repetitive* occurrence of similar feet or similar combinations of feet (as it must, since *any* piece of language can be scanned), then Gioia's observation that free verse is *more* regular than it might appear combines with Steele's that traditional verse is *less* regular than it might appear, implying that any difference between metered and unmetered verse will be a difference of degree rather than kind. Strict repetition—too much meter—produces doggerel, and unconstrained variety—too little meter—produces prose. Verse, suspended between regular and irregular rhythm, depends on the tension between variety and repetition. Postmodernists and New Formalists alike employ that tension.

As a corrective to this misconception I recommend a revision of Roethke's precept: "Say to yourself: I will learn and treasure every [vibrant form] ever made." New Formalism need not grant postmodern poetry a monopoly on formal experimentation and need not trap itself within a confining concept of form. A postmodernist would be wrong to think that traditional forms have lost their power, but a New Formalist would err in believing that only *traditional* forms are formal.

MISCONCEPTION 2: New Formalism Returns Poetry to the Populace; Postmodernism Imprisons It in Universities

This misconception, like the first, absolutizes both sides of a comparison until it becomes a false dilemma. Certainly New Formalism has sought to restore elements that characterized poetry in an era during which it was disseminated primarily through means other than universities (such as newspapers and oral tradition). But the relation between campus and culture has changed, as has the relation between culture and the media. A vastly higher percentage of the citizenry attend college now than did so prior to modernism, for reasons having to do more immediately with social phenomena such as feminism and the GI Bill than with the ideological tenets of modernism. This changing dynamic has affected other fields in addition to poetry: for instance, naturalists like Darwin and Audubon once operated outside of universities, but biological investigation now occurs almost exclusively in universities.

Thus, if both New Formalist and postmodernist poets want to reach a broadly based audience of thoughtful, intelligent citizens, the sort who read the *Atlantic* and *Harper's* in preference to *People* and who watch *Washington Week in Review* in preference to *World's Wildest Police Videos*, then one of the primary avenues for "catching" that audience will be the university, since so many members of that audience pass through it.

I take as implied by this observation the recommendation that New Formalism not burn its bridges to the university. In its maturation process, New Formalism needs self-consciously to avoid too quickly settling its self-image, by inviting ongoing critical dialogue—including, and especially, dissenting views—from all points, whether that dialogue occurs in a coffeehouse or a college classroom. Postmodernist poetry needs an audience off campus no less than does New Formalist poetry, and New Formalist poetry needs an audience on campus no less than does postmodernist poetry.

MISCONCEPTION 3: New Formalists Must Reject Postmodern Poetry

One need not agree with Marjorie Perloff's assessment of poetry to learn from her version of why poetry's audience has assumed its current membership and adopted its present posture, nor need one adopt postmodernist theories or styles to learn from them. Postmodernism offers enough fecund ideas and engaging poets that dismissing postmodernism can only impoverish a reader. Even putting aside the best work of theorists who are not poets (works like Baudrillard's *The Ecstasy of Communication* or Lyotard's *The Differend*), plenty of important thought remains. Charles Bernstein's "Artifice of Absorption," for example, offers a meditation on the relation between form and meaning that any New Formalist would find edifying. And a comparison between the way Rosmarie Waldrop uses quotation in *The Reproduction of Profiles* and the way R. S. Gwynn uses quotation in "Approaching a Significant Birthday, He Peruses *The Norton Anthology of Poetry*" would benefit any thoughtful reader or aspiring poet.

My final inference, then, modifies the Heraclitean maxim about harmony depending on tension, recommending that we resist tradition even as we employ it, that we find and assimilate the pleasures and wisdom available outside the tradition one finds most familiar. If you identify yourself with New Formalism, spend some time with Susan Howe and Michael Palmer. Buy Story Line books until your nightstand will hold no more, but back them up with books from The Figures and Lost Roads and Sun and Moon. If you identify with L=A=N=G=U=A=G=E poetry, try a little Rachel Hadas. To understand and honor a wide range of approaches to poetry can enliven one's own approach. The dynamic *tension* between traditional forms and nontraditional, between New Formalist and postmodern, can be vivifying and productive.

New Formalism at
a Crossroads

The nearly simultaneous release of three synoptic books of criticism from Story Line Press, the primary publishing organ for New Formalist poetry, signals an urgency within New Formalism to answer for itself and its (envisioned) public the old Greek interrogative greeting: "Where have you been and where are you going?" Kevin Walzer's monograph *The Ghost of Tradition: Expansive Poetry and Postmodernism* and R. S. Gwynn's anthology *New Expansive Poetry: Theory, Criticism, History* focus on the "where have you been" part of the question, while Annie Finch's anthology *After New Formalism: Poets on Form, Narrative, and Tradition* addresses the "where are you going" part.

The two parts of the question relate to two opposed imperatives literary criticism must balance: to offer full and accurate description, which readers and writers need as pilots need weather reports and as hikers need topographical maps; and to reconceptualize and recontextualize, because for readers and writers, unlike pilots and to an order of magnitude beyond hikers, safe arrival at a destination matters less than achieving a reorienting vision of the world. Each imperative entices toward a trap: a map oversimplifies the landscape and presents it as static; a reconceptualization substitutes the ideal for the real. Pursuing either imperative exclusively enforces failure, and the two imperatives contradict each other. But paradox has never negated obligation, so criticism must simultaneously settle and unsettle. In this case, since

New Formalism's current crisis arises from the danger of becoming settled too surely too soon, it takes no Aristotle to discern that these three books succeed to the degree that they err on the side of unsettling their object, contesting its space more than plotting it. By such a measure their order of relative success and importance ascends from Walzer through Gwynn to Finch.

In the first paragraph of his preface, Walzer identifies for his book three goals, each important to the assessment of where New Formalism has been. *The Ghost of Tradition* aims, he says, first "to note the history and growing achievement of the movement" that he calls "Expansive poetry," second to "examine the work of its more significant poets," and finally to speculate "on the movement's influence on contemporary poetry" and on literary history. The brief opening chapter concentrates on the first goal, the second and seventh chapters concentrate on the third goal, and the intervening chapters concentrate on the second goal.

The first chapter's historical narrative identifies three publications—"a 1988 issue of *Crosscurrents*, edited by Dick Allen, a 1989 anthology of essays, *Expansive Poetry*, edited by Frederick Feirstein, and a 1990 issue of *Verse*, edited by Robert McPhillips"—as the primary occasions for the movement's initial self-identification, and *Rebel Angels*, Mark Jarman's and David Mason's anthology, as the vehicle of its first significant consolidation.

The second chapter of *The Ghost of Tradition* argues that the dominance of "Postmodernist thought" in universities has meant that "Language poetry," due to "its oppositional stance," has enjoyed a warm reception by university writers and critics, while Expansive poetry, because of its use of tradition, has suffered a hostile reception in the form of an unfair dismissal as reactionary. The dismissal's unfairness lies, according to Walzer, in failure to observe how significantly the Expansive poets differ from their Formalist predecessors: their frequent adoption of liberal ideologies and pop-cultural subjects lets them put "traditional aesthetics to Postmodern use." As a result, Expansive poetry, on Walzer's view, simultaneously "is Postmodern" and "contains an implicit critique of mainstream Postmodern thought."

Walzer's central chapters attend to the work of fifteen poets, offering readings of Dana Gioia, David Mason, Robert McDowell, and Mary Jo Salter as poets who "use beautiful surfaces to explore deeper human stories and subjects"; of Mark Jarman, Marilyn Nelson, Molly Peacock, and Frederick Turner as poets who "paint in bold colors"; of Emily Grosholz, Rachel Hadas, and Timothy Steele as poets who "challenge the identification of lyric with free verse" and work "effectively in a variety of forms to address a number of contemporary subjects and themes"; and of Thomas Disch, Frederick Feirstein, R. S. Gwynn, and Charles Martin as poets who have "revived the tradition of satiric, discursive poetry."

Walzer concludes that Expansive poetry's achievements include "extending the range of possibilities of style and subject in contemporary poetry," producing "an accessible body of criticism that challenges" postmodernism, and "arguing for poetry's emergence from an academic subculture to a position of greater importance in American life."

Because they are anthologies, the Gwynn and Finch books lend themselves to briefer descriptions. Gwynn's *New Expansive Poetry* updates a previous anthology, Frederick Feirstein's 1989 volume *Expansive Poetry: Essays on New Narrative and New Formalism*. Gwynn's introduction links the need to update Feirstein's volume to developments that have altered two canons: the general canon of contemporary literature, and the more specific canon of "Expansive poetry" itself. According to Gwynn, the ten years since Feirstein's anthology "have witnessed the arrival of the poets and poetry it championed at a secure place" in the general canon of contemporary literature. The poets have "prospered to a degree that has surpassed the expectations of even their most ardent early supporters." More narrowly, within Expansive poetry itself, the canon has formed far more fully than it had ten years ago: then the new narrative canon could "boast only a handful" of successful poems, and "New Formalism lacked any defining anthologies . . . by which readers could judge its merits," but since then such narrative poems as Mark Jarman's *Iris*, Robert McDowell's *The Diviners*, and David Mason's "The Country I Remember" have appeared, as have two widely read anthologies, Annie Finch's *A Formal Feeling Comes* and Jarman's and Mason's *Rebel Angels*.

Gwynn adopts the division into "New Formalism" and "new narrative" as the book's defining structural element, treating those two categories as subsets of "expansive poetry." He includes a number of essays from the Feirstein anthology but adds "standards" such as Brad Leithauser's "Metrical Illiteracy" along with important contextualizing work such as Meg Schoerke's illuminating comparison of New Formalist criticism to the early twentieth-century debate over free verse. In addition, Gwynn includes statements from poets represented in Annie Finch's first anthology, *A Formal Feeling Comes: Poems in Form by Contemporary Women*.

Finch's current contribution to New Formalism's self-assessment, *After New Formalism*, pursues a different end from Walzer's book or Gwynn's. Finch's book, like their books, still acts as "in a sense an archaeological endeavor," but she alters her emphasis "to include thoughtful essays by poets engaging with formalism from outside its confines, as well as by younger poets who came to formalism with a more theoretical bent than their elders." Whatever the direction of any given essay in the anthology, Finch wants the assortment as a whole to represent her "own vision of a 'multiformalism' that truly encompasses the many formal poetic traditions, including experimental traditions, now native to the United States."

Finch includes many of the same poets discussed by Walzer and included by Gwynn. Eight poets (Frederick Feirstein, Dana Gioia, Mark Jarman, David Mason, Marilyn Nelson, Molly Peacock, Timothy Steele, and Frederick Turner) enjoy significant space in all three books: part of a chapter in Walzer and an essay in Gwynn and Finch. Several other figures get space in two of the three books: Thomas M. Disch, Paul Lake, Robert McPhillips, and Mary Jo Salter, along with Gwynn and Finch themselves. But the individuals represented in only one of the books are in the case of Walzer and Gwynn primarily figures who have been associated frequently with New Formalism already (Robert McDowell and Emily Grosholz, for example, in Walzer; Wyatt Prunty and Brad Leithauser in Gwynn), while Finch's singles include several surprises, among them Adrienne Rich, Carolyn Beard Whitlow, Agha Shahid Ali, and Amittai Aviram.

Each book explicitly recognizes what the combination of the three implicitly confirms: that New Formalism stands at a significant crossroads. After enumerating its achievements, Walzer says that Expansive poetry "may have already done all it can do to transform the way we read and think about American poetry," leaving it with a single charge, "the most important work of poets: writing memorable poems." Gwynn begins his preface with the achievements of New Formalism but ends with an ongoing challenge to "force and elegance" sounded two decades ago by Richard Wilbur "like advice for a prophet who had not yet arrived" and yet to be adequately fulfilled. Finch, advocating her own view of "multiformalism," celebrates the degree to which "discourse about formalism changed" during the time she spent editing the book, and calls for "much more critical attention to forms from other than European traditions as well as to the procedural and other forms used by 'experimental' poets."

In identifying this moment as a crucial one, and in fulfillment of criticism's twin calls to settle and to unsettle, the books raise a series of issues that suggest possible paths for New Formalism. The magnitude of the decisions New Formalism faces stands revealed in the questions the three books raise, to pause over and puzzle through which would enrich any reader, and responses to which will help determine New Formalism's future direction(s). A few such issues follow, each paused over briefly.

1: Can New Formalism Construct a Durable, Flexible Identity?

Consensus on the core group of eight poets represented in all three books masks a lack of clarity about the underlying basis of the consensus and therefore a lack of clarity about the identity of New Formalism. Why these poets and not others? Haziness on that issue leads to peculiar moments in Walzer, as when, in describing Marilyn Nelson's work, he suggests that only one of her books exemplifies form and narrative in full flower, or when, having affirmed in Chapter 1 that new narrative poetry follows the "conventions of realistic narrative, in which the entire story is told," he praises Robert McDowell's poems for their episodic nature, their telling only small portions of a tale and leaving "the rest of the life . . . to speculation." An account of the role of poetic development and a more subtle theory of narrative (like Meir Sternberg's tension between the truth and the whole truth) might better explain the inclusion of these poets in preference to others and would generate a correspondingly richer apology for New Formalist poetry.

If consensus on the poets themselves has priority, membership will be durable and the criteria for membership will adapt to identify the given membership. But that kevorkial prescription would guarantee the movement's death. If in ten years membership remains the same, with all the same poets and only the same poets dominating that era's New Formalist anthologies, the signal will be not that New Formalism stands at a crossroads but that it lies in a grave. If, in contrast, a durable basis for consensus can be clarified, then membership can be flexible and open-ended, allowing the best newer voices to join the best older ones. In that case, New Formalism would identify an approach to poetic practice. Giving priority to the underlying principles will keep the movement dynamic; giving priority to the individuals identified with the movement will make it static.

The most conspicuous signal of the lack of clarity about the identity of New Formalism is the disagreement between the three books over the best name for the object of their attention: Walzer and Gwynn use "Expansive poetry" and Finch "New Formalism." The infelicitous title of the Gwynn anthology adds to the mess: though he must mean "a new version of the previous anthology on Expansive poetry," the title reads as if it christens the movement "new Expansive poetry." Neither candidate is as catchy as "the Beats"; "Expansive poetry" is even more pretentious and nebulous than the name of its nemesis "language poetry"; "New Formalism" seems to slight poets who emphasize narrative; and neither term names the locale for the poets' association as "the Black Mountain poets" does (though on a forgiving chronology "the West Chester poets" might serve). In the absence of better candidates, the wider acceptance of "New Formalism," its having both an adjectival and a nominative form ("Expansive poetry" = "New Formalist poetry," but "Expansion" won't work the way "New Formalism" does), and its at least approaching the descriptive character of a term like "confessional poets" urge its acceptance.

2: How Will New Formalism Relate to Other Currents in Contemporary Poetry and Culture?

Straightforward opposition may have been a useful stance in establishing the initial granfalloon, but will not serve New Formalism well as an ongoing relation to other elements of culture.

Walzer is weakest on this point. If I could alter any part of any one of these books, I would wish away the "and Postmodernism" from Walzer's title and text, for several reasons.

• By taking Jameson for the whole of postmodern theory and Perloff and Byers for the whole of postmodern critical practice, Walzer argues against a straw person, and a flimsy one at that. Because *The Ghost of Tradition* appears not to understand postmodernism, nor want to, the book adopts a prejudicial air that Walzer's sometimes illuminating readings of individual poems should not be forced to overcome.

• By replicating the same false dilemma he attributes to the postmoderns (either Formalism or postmodernism), Walzer commits the same "reduction" to "monolith" that they commit. Ironically, Walzer's book tacitly calls for what Derrida designates a "deconstruction": not "passing from one concept to another," but "overturning and displacing a conceptual order, as well as the nonconceptual order with which the conceptual order is articulated."

• Walzer *says* New Formalism is a continuation of Formalism and critique of postmodernism but then shows it as a combination of the two. New Formalism's inclusion of pop culture, for instance, distinguishes it from earlier Formalism and allies it with postmodernism. More fully developing this richer and more complex view would show Walzer's other insights to better advantage.

To define New Formalism primarily by reference to another movement misstates its achievements and underestimates its potential. On this issue, the two anthologies, which present New Formalism with less dependence on a prior, opposed movement as foil, depict New Formalism with more insight.

3: What Lends Rhyme, Meter, and Narrative the Privilege New Formalism Attributes to Them?

The most challenging essay in any of the books, Frederick Turner's and Ernst Pöppel's "The Neural Lyre: Poetic Meter, the Brain, and Time" in the Gwynn anthology, attempts to answer Question 3. The central thesis Turner and Pöppel assert—that poetic meter results inevitably from the human brain's physiology and provides the ultimate vehicle for human cognition—is false, and their essay suffers the flaws of any natural-law argument. But that hardly matters. As John Kekes has pointed out, a theory can be deep without being true, as for instance Freud's theories show. Others have asserted versions of Turner's and Pöppel's thesis before, as Peter Viereck did a few years ago. But unlike Viereck's embarrassingly shallow view (the heart goes ta-tum ta-tum and we have five fingers on each hand, so nature urges us to write in iambic pentameter), Turner and Pöppel offer an exhilarating, even dizzying, concatenation of anthropological, physiological, and philosophical perspectives, and the depth of their view will enliven any reader's view of the importance of meter.

Timothy Steele substitutes an appeal to history for the Turner/Pöppel appeal to science. Steele argues that the fathers of free verse (Ford, Pound, and Eliot in his genealogy) mistook their "revolution" as "an innovation of the sort which inevitably accompanies changes in style and taste." They failed to understand that, "historically considered, non-metrical verse is nothing if not singular, in that, until this century, virtually all Western poetry is informed by the distinction," made by Gorgias and Aristotle, "that prose is organized in the general patterns and periods of rhythm (*rhythmos*) and poetry in the specifically and regularly ordered rhythmical units of meter (*metron*)." The basic motive that urged Pound and his puppies to purge their poems was good: Victorian verse had grown decadent. But instead of changing "from one clear set of principles to another," they tried to make "an escape from metric" altogether, and neither of their hoped-for consequences—an emergence of new forms or a revival of the old—happened. Instead, "several generations of poets have merely continued to write non-metrically." Though Steele steers a more cautious course than Turner and Pöppel do, his appeal to tradition—we always wrote that way before—cannot ground rhyme, meter, and narrative any more than can their appeal to nature. But his essay, like theirs, has depth: it urges an exacting approach to literary history and challenges poets to reaffirm the standards of craft Steele considers implicit in meter.

The recurring critiques of modernism in these three books, echoing in the empty space created by the conspicuous absence of a satisfying *apologia pro forma sua*, announce a need. If Dana Gioia is New Formalism's Pound, the poet/critic who has articulated a powerful revisionist view of literary history and who excels at identifying and championing new talent, and Robert McDowell its Laughlin, the poet/publisher able to offer the movement's work to a broad reading public, the reticence of these three books on the issue of the source of form's force reveals that New Formalism still wants its Eliot to send down in prose and verse a philosophical taproot to let the tree grow tall.

4: How Does, or How Can, New Formalism Accommodate a Wealth of New and Various Voices?

Walzer, Gwynn, and Finch agree that New Formalism has legitimated itself as a presence in American poetry. Not only does it have its own journals, presses, and conferences but, more important, it has begun to exert influence beyond its own borders: sonnets have proliferated in other journals and books and even in the workshops New Formalist rhetoric impugns. But the same threat that attends legitimacy in any movement—whether literary or political or religious—now faces New Formalism. The transition from idiolect (from the Greek *lexis*, for word, from *legein*, to speak) to legitimacy (from the Latin *lex*, for law) purchases acceptance, but at the price of autonomy.

For its force to persist, New Formalism will need to internalize its dialogue (*dialegesthai*, from *legein*) in order to avoid becoming doctrinaire, letting the laws limit the words, atrophying the work. In helping New Formalism toward this transition from arguing against others to a lively internal debate, both anthology editors have excelled. Gwynn's anthology by its very being engages Feirstein's earlier edition. Gwynn's changes also make the dialogue more reflective: the important addition of women's statements from *A Formal Feeling Comes*, the perspective added by the Schoerke essay, and the moderation of David Mason's essay on shorter narrative all help the voice crying in the wilderness modulate a little toward talking to itself. In the end, the lasting public impact for which New Formalism so expressly longs will happen more through the E. F. Hutton effect than through stentorian calls to revolution. Make a conversation interesting enough, and people will listen in.

Finch's anthology takes an even more energetic approach than Gwynn's to the necessary transition. Its wider range of voices enriches its resonances, including its resonances with the Gwynn anthology. For instance, Finch includes a powerful—and unsettling—essay by Marilyn Nelson about the meaning of tradition for a black woman. If Timothy Steele's essay in the Gwynn anthology asks why we have abandoned the tradition, Nelson's in the Finch anthology asks: "Why don't we . . . take possession of, why don't we own, the tradition? Own the masters, all of them." Same question, but the different "we" gives it a different flavor, and having both questions on the table in counterpoint adds a dimension to each. *There* is a conversation worth having: if New Formalism wants a public presence, that is the sort of discussion that will earn one.

Similarly, Amittai Aviram's essay on rhythm (in Finch) challenges Steele's assertion (in Gwynn) that meter defines poetry and rhythm defines prose. Aviram's account of what distinguishes poetry from prose gives him a different starting place. According to Aviram, "what makes poetry distinct from prose, and what offers to poetry-lovers a pleasure not available elsewhere, is the fact that poetry does not consist entirely in meaning. Poetry is experienced simultaneously as a meaningful utterance and as a play of sounds." His diagnosis of the problem also differs from Steele's: Aviram emphasizes the equivocation on the word "free" that has led to a widely held, mistaken view that "free" verse is free not only in a technical sense but in a political sense as well. Even though Steele and Aviram agree in advocating a revitalization of metrical verse as the treatment for poetry's ills, Aviram's prescription does not match Steele's: Aviram advocates "standing the conventional view on its head: making meaning subordinate to rhythm." As with Marilyn Nelson's essay versus Steele's, so with Aviram's versus Steele's: the dialogue between the two enriches both.

5. What History Will New Formalism Claim for Itself?

The hyperbolic assertion, important to the New-Formalism-as-rebellion version of its history, that during the sixties, seventies, and eighties free verse had complete control of the poetry world, nearly eliminating formal poetry in an act of aesthetic cleansing, sounds a false note, the tinny clang of conspiracy theory. John Hollander, Anthony Hecht, James Merrill, and others were publishing with the best house. Howard Moss was editing the *New Yorker*. And the list of Pulitzers in any twenty-year period since its inception has featured a majority of poets writing in traditional form. Even in the depths of the purported reign of free verse, the 1970s and 1980s, the prize went to more narrative and Formalist poets than not: Richard Howard, James Merrill, Howard Nemerov, and Donald Justice among them. Pulitzer score: Richard Wilbur 2, Robert Bly 0. The famine may have been visible, with the hungry in the streets, but (as Amartya Sen points out) famine arises not from insufficient food supply but from the food's becoming too expensive for the poor to purchase. The wealthy never starve, and Formalists have eaten well in every decade.

Of the two books focused on New Formalism's history, Gwynn's gives by far the more robust, and Walzer's the more anemic, answer to the "where have you been" question, in part—and paradoxically—because Gwynn fails at the implied aim of canon-fixing, and Walzer succeeds. The reason for the paradox is simple: it is too soon to fix the canon. It is *always* too soon to fix the canon of literature in general, and certainly this early stage in New Formalism's development is too soon to fix its specific canon, for the reasons suggested above. Any group of affiliates, from a high-school clique to a religious denomination, will need to posit criteria that define its membership and establish its difference from other groups, but closed membership ensures a static group. In order to achieve the aim that leads some of its proponents to call this group "Expansive" poets, New Formalism must sustain a dynamic tension between self-definition and openness. The more conclusively New Formalism settles on its own canon, the weaker will be that dynamic tension, and the weaker its dynamism, the more New Formalism will resemble a corpse.

Walzer repeats the story the "first generation" New Formalists told about their ordeals: that they struggled against the monolithic university creative writing establishment to slay the dragon of free verse, enduring persecution along the way for their righteous faith in form. That Platonic "noble lie" may have helped to unify and direct the energies of those poets, but it cannot stand scrutiny. The story of New Formalism as rebellion, in fact, helped cause the current dilemma. Rebels can stay rebels only as long as they lose; when they win (and the consensus of these three books seems to be that, in New Formalism's case, they have), rebels can only assume the role they previously defined as evil. New Formalism would be better served to discard the narrative of rebellion and adopt a history that defines it independently of the equation winner/tyrant, loser/rebel. Recusancy, heresy, disavowal, displacement, differend, all function across a wider range of conditions than rebellion can, and each offers a more satisfying ideal than rebellion.

6. Can New Formalism Create an Understanding of Form that Is Rich and Various Enough to Identify and Further the Best New Poetry Being Written?

More than any other factor, the answer to this question will determine whether New Formalism withers or thrives. New Formalism's originating gesture, the reversal of a decline in the production of poetry that employs meter and narrative in traditional ways and of a widespread neglect of study of traditional forms, *was* in its moment "expansive." It broadened the range of practice and discourse about poetry. Now New Formalism must face a different situation and adapt itself in order to continue being "expansive." The same advocacy of rhyme, meter, and narrative that reopened those possibilities for poets can be used now to *close* other possibilities, but New Formalism must resist the temptation to do so.

One way to maintain an expansive posture in New Formalism is suggested by Timothy Steele, this time in his essay from the Finch anthology rather than the essay in Gwynn. In "Boundless Wealth from a Finite Store: Meter and Grammar," Steele explores the "crucial point" that "poetry consists neither exclusively of grammatical prose-sense nor exclusively of meter, but is rather a fusion of the two." He advocates hearing in poems "both their grammatical and their metrical structures," but in doing so he makes another point, equally crucial to New Formalism now: meter is far more "varied and complex" than our usual categorizations capture. It was important to New Formalism's beginnings to emphasize the regularity of meter in contradistinction to the irregularity of prose. But Steele shows that meter's strengths derive from *ir*regularities. His careful scrutiny of numerous examples necessitates an expansion of the usual distinction between stressed/unstressed syllables into a distinction between four levels of stress. So Sidney's "Milk hands, rose cheeks, or lips more sweet, more red," alternates between heavily stressed and very heavily stressed syllables, in a pattern Steele numbers as 3 4 3 4 1 4 3 4 3 4, unlike Frost's "The clouds were low and hairy in the skies," which Steele hears as 1 4 1 4 1 4 1 2 1 4. Q: When is iambic pentameter not iambic pentameter? A: Always. New Formalism has helped to show that free verse was never free, and now needs to explore (*not* to deny or cover over) the consequences of a related fact: that "regular" meter always was free verse.

New Formalism must decide whether to replicate fractally the failure Dana Gioia has attributed to poetry itself, by becoming a subculture within the subculture of poetry, or to adopt the attitude of the Cornelius Eady poem cited by Marilyn Nelson in the Finch anthology, becoming "a brick in a house / that is being built / around your house." New Formalism must decide whether to settle for a narrow, fundamentalist view of form or to commit to the ongoing challenge of remaining "expansive" in its understanding of form and of form's infinite possibilities.

The most dynamic visions of New Formalism remain Dana Gioia's call for a restoration of the fullness of poetry's generic possibilities and Annie Finch's "multiformalism," because both of these visions serve to *un*settle more than to settle. If the Walzer, Gwynn, and Finch books can prompt New Formalism toward the ecumenical turn such views offer, they will have performed a great service for New Formalism and for contemporary poetry.

Formal Experimentation and Poetic Discovery

Great poems speak with greater wisdom than the poets who wrote them possessed. The catalysis for such alchemy comes from form.

In saying so, I mean to dispute the common assumption that poetry serves primarily as self-expression. Construing poetry as a vehicle for self-expression stunts individual poems and too narrowly restricts the range of poetry itself. Any poem may tell something the poet already knows, allowing the poet to instruct other readers, but a rich poem also reveals things the poet did not know, thereby edifying all its readers, the poet included.

The anesthetic uniformity of so much contemporary American poetry, for which the proliferation of M.F.A. programs has taken disproportionate and often misguided blame, results less from the increasingly isomorphic educational background of the poets—there is nothing wrong with the M.F.A. *per se*—than from the pervasiveness of the assumption that poetry functions primarily as a vehicle for self-expression. What fault falls rightly on creative writing degrees lies not in the fact of the programs but in the frequency with which they inculcate a confining and homogenizing—and ultimately shallow—premise about the process and the aim of writing a poem. "What's dull," Marina Tsvetaeva asserts, "is not the monotony, but the fact that the thing repeated—though it may be very varied—is insignificant."

Self-expression gained ideological currency in a specific cultural context, in which it could be understood as revelatory. At its origin in the Enlightenment, the ideal of self-expression, as Kathleen Higgins observes, reflected "both Enlightenment glorification of the universal and the Kantian emphasis on the subjective character of experience," and depended on the then-predominant psychological view that humans possess "a universal self, free from the empirical constraints and practical motives that distinguish one person from another." In our day, though, the diminished plausibility of such a psychology makes it difficult to find a non-self-indulgent purpose for self-expression to fulfill and impossible to consider self-expression *per se* as revelatory of anything that might matter to others. Had I a universal self (with capacities that mimic God's), my expression of that self would necessarily possess the nature of revelation, different from divine revelation only in degree but not in kind; absent so elevated a self, my self-expression may offer me relief (hence its function in psychotherapy) but cannot, without help, offer anyone else edification.

Put another way, self-expression by an Enlightenment universal self would bump the poem up Northrop Frye's ladder of fictional modes toward Romance, in which the protagonist (the narrator in a case of self-expression) exceeds other humans, or even toward myth, in which the protagonist is divine; but self-expression in the absence of a universal self could only drag the poem down the ladder from low mimesis (in which the protagonist is just "one of us") toward irony (in which the protagonist is less capable than others). The incompleteness and tendentiousness of my point of view in regard to my nonuniversal self means that self-expression *simpliciter* can only expose my flaws. As I am now, without a universal self, simple self-expression fits me less to function as an oracle than as a guest on *Jerry Springer*.

Pursued as the focal ambition of a poem or posited as its defining ideal, self-expression forfeits revelation. But revelation remains a poetic *sine qua non*, as George Oppen, in his usual incisive way, declares: "I think that poetry which is of any value is *always* revelatory. Not that it reveals or could reveal Everything, but it must reveal something (I would like to say 'Something' and for the first time)." To reveal something, for the first time or not, demands some *means* of discovery.

Without help from the gods, the muses, or the universal self, form offers the most viable means of poetic discovery.

Form might initiate discovery in any of several different ways. William H. Gass observes, for instance, that form works like 3-D glasses to open poetic space: "Musical form creates another syntax, which overlaps the grammatical and reinforces that set of directions sometimes, or adds another dimension by suggesting that two words, when they alliterate or rhyme, thereby modify each other, even if they are not in any normally modifying position. Everything a sentence is is made manifest by its music." Joseph Brodsky describes a different mechanism, in which form provides a prompt that prevents passivity in thought, thus extending the Wittgensteinian unbounded visual field that represents life's limitlessness. "A poet," Brodsky says, "is someone for whom every word is not the end but the beginning of a thought; someone who, having uttered *rai* ('paradise') or *tot svet* ('next world'), must mentally take the subsequent step of finding a rhyme for it. Thus *krai* ('edge/realm') and *otsvet* ('reflection') emerge, and the existence of those whose life has ended is prolonged."

Here, though, I want to focus not on the whole of form as a means of poetic discovery, which, like Zarathustra's leech, would be too much for me, but more narrowly on formal *experimentation* as a means. Consider Elizabeth Bishop's "Visits to St. Elizabeths," a poem that experiments with a form significantly different from any other in Bishop's oeuvre, beginning with the simple declarative "This is the house of Bedlam," and building through repetition, variation, and addition to this complex final stanza:

> This is the soldier home from the war.
> These are the years and the walls and the door
> that shut on a boy that pats the floor
> to see if the world is round or flat.
> This is a Jew in a newspaper hat
> that dances carefully down the ward,
> walking the plank of a coffin board
> with the crazy sailor
> that shows his watch
> that tells the time

of the wretched man
that lies in the house of Bedlam.

Many Bishop poems employ traditional metrical patterns and center around detailed observation. "Sandpiper," which appears near "Visits to St. Elizabeths" in the same section of *Questions of Travel*, can serve as a representative Bishop poem. Each quatrain uses either an *abab* rhyme or a rhyme scheme that supports the *abab* even as it diverges from it slightly: one stanza uses an *abbb* scheme, and another an *abcb* scheme. The meter varies, but it varies from an iambic pentameter base. Bishop depicts her subject, the small shore bird called a sand-piper, in its instinctive food-gathering, using its beak between waves to gather morsels from the sand of the littoral zone: "The beach hisses like fat. On his left, a sheet / of interrupting water comes and goes / and glazes over his dark and brittle feet. / He runs, he runs straight through it, watching his toes." The poem's eye for detail depicts the value and states the limitations of an eye for detail: "The world is a mist. And then the world is / minute and vast and clear. The tide / is higher or lower. He couldn't tell you which. / His beak is focussed; he is preoccupied."

"Sandpiper" shares with "The Fish" its attention to an animal as subject. "The Fish" shares with "The Armadillo" its Brazilian setting. "The Armadillo" and "Over 2,000 Illustrations and a Complete Concordance" share careful observation of the activities of those to whose countries the poet has traveled. If no two Bishop poems are exactly alike, nearly any two will share something substantial in common. Even a prose poem such as "12 O'Clock News" has sisters. "Visits to St. Elizabeths," though, seems anomalous, utterly unlike any other Bishop poem.

In fact, it seems unlike any other poem, period. Many poets have portrayed institutionalized individuals, themselves included. From Christopher Smart's "Jubilate Agno" to Theodore Roethke's "Heard in a Violent Ward," institutionalized madness has been fodder for poetry. But "idiot" and "idiom" share a root, and each such poem serves (as madness says it must) as a law unto itself. Even within the subclass defined by its subject, Bishop's poem has no siblings. For example, Louise Bogan's "Evening in the Sanitarium" achieves its unsettling effects through long lines, anesthetic tone, and "obsessive" imagery:

The free evening fades, outside the windows fastened with
  decorative iron grilles.
The lamps are lighted; the shades drawn; the nurses are
  watching a little.
It is the hour of the complicated knitting on the safe bone
  needles; of the games of anagrams and bridge;
The deadly game of chess; the book held up like a mask.

Bogan's poem is depressive, filled with gloomy fixations, but Bishop's is manic, circling wildly around itself.

"Visits to St. Elizabeths" does not assume a "regular" stanza form, but begins with a single isolated line, and adds to it a line per stanza: "This is the house of Bedlam. // This is the man / that lies in the house of Bedlam. // This is the time / of the tragic man / that lies in the house of Bedlam." And so on. The accretion, of course, creates part of the poem's meaning, conveying the sense of rapidly increasing burden that leads to, or that allows us to identify with, insanity. A poem like Jason Sommer's "Last in before Dark" portrays the benign version of this insistent, ongoing accumulation of the burdens of life; "Visits to St. Elizabeths" portrays the malignant version.

The poem's accretive form resembles that of certain children's songs, such as "This Is the House that Jack Built," or the song my paternal grandmother taught me: "There's a hole in the bottom of the sea. / There's a log on the hole in the bottom of the sea. / There's a knot on the log on the hole in the bottom of the sea. / There's a frog on the knot on the log on the hole in the bottom of the sea. / There's a wart on the frog on the knot on the log on the hole in the bottom of the sea." And so on. The resemblance itself contributes to the meaning of the poem, since many forms of madness share as a characteristic the restoration of some childlike attributes, an infantilization of the adult.

Another aspect of the form Bishop uses—repetition with variation—functions as a staple of music. Its most visible presence in poetry occurs in French forms like the villanelle, the ballade, and others, but repetition with variation also informs smaller, elemental units of poetry such as rhyme and alliteration. In "Visits to St. Elizabeths," some lines are repeated numerous times, but the variations give significance. For example, "the man / that lies in the house of Bedlam" becomes "the tragic man," "the talkative man," "the honored man," "the old, brave man," "the cranky man," and so on. And the Jew who usually "dances weeping down the ward" appears in the last two stanzas dancing first "joyfully" and then "carefully." The whirling, disorienting sensation produced by the frequent repetitions and subtle variations mimics madness in the reader in a way that description in some other form could not.

The nature of a poet's formal experimentation may vary, as may the place experimental work holds in a poet's corpus. Experimentation can manipulate characteristics as simple as scale: "The Wreck of the Deutschland" surely exemplifies formal experimentation that brings discovery, even though it uses "sprung rhythm" just like Hopkins's (shorter) sonnets. Certainly formal experimentation need not have as its focus traditional rhyme and meter. George Oppen's "Of Being Numerous" experiments (like Hopkins's "Wreck") with scale, consisting of forty numbered sections of unrhymed verse in irregular meter. Here the scale and the numbering clearly embody thematic concerns, exhorting the reader to fulfill the ideal stated within the poem: "One must not come to feel that he has a thousand threads in his hands, / He must somehow see the one thing."

Formal experimentation of the sort Bishop undertakes in "Visits to St. Elizabeths" might mark a turning point in a poet's career, establishing the "experimental" form as the norm for the poet, as happens in a poem such as "The Crossroads of the World Etc.," the poem from *The Moving Target* in which W. S. Merwin abandons punctuation for good. The experimentation in such a case accomplishes a "conversion" for the poet. But the influence of formal experimentation need not be so abrupt and transparent. In some cases, like Josephine Miles's *Kinds of Affection* or Donald Hall's *The One Day*, the poets' taking a new formal path did not result in their staying on the new path permanently, only in their returning invigorated to a prior path. In still other cases, the experimentation may be simply an aberration with no discernible future influence or consequences, as in C. K. Williams's "Villanelle."

The revelatory power of formal experimentation does not confine itself to poetry but recapitulates itself in society at large. Modernism, for example, can be construed as a discovery of new formal possibilities. Indeed, in retrospect, stages of history reveal themselves as more or less integrated modifications of society's understanding of natural form, of the political and economic forms society elects, the literary and artistic forms it creates and values, the forms of its kinship structures, and so on, as shown by books such as C. S. Lewis's *The Discarded Image*, E. M. W. Tillyard's *The Elizabethan World Picture*, and Octavio Paz's *The Other Voice*.

By a string of associations, through its loose synonym "style" to that word's homonym "stile," we may define "form" as an arrangement of steps that enables passage across a boundary that the steps themselves help to define. Just as in science the purpose of experimentation—to verify or disprove hypotheses—is clear, so is the purpose of formal experimentation clear in poetry: it enables the poet to defy her own limitations of intelligence, knowledge, and point of view and thus to discover and reveal what she did not already know. To quote Tsvetaeva once more: "Every poem is an utterance of the Sibyl—infinitely more than was said by the tongue."

On the (Ir)Regularity
of Meter

One dynamic in recent American poetry has been the nearly simultaneous efflorescence of New Formalism and L=A=N=G=U=A=G=E
poetry. The differences between the two opposed perspectives extend
to nearly every possible issue: the connection or separation between
poetry and politics, the relation of poetry to academic institutions, who
were the best poets of the past, and so on. Certainly one important
point of disagreement between the two camps is formal and has to do
with the role of meter. Here I will attempt to reconcile the two schools
on that point by contrasting what Timothy Steele (considered a leading
proponent of New Formalism) says on the matter with what Charles
Bernstein (a leading proponent of L=A=N=G=U=A=G=E poetry) says,
not attempting to *ally* the two views, but to *alloy* one with the other in
order to construct an alternative.

Timothy Steele's *Missing Measures* makes a compelling case for
traditional metrical values in English-language poetry, and his acuity in
observing and articulating the problems of modernism places *Missing
Measures* among the very best works of criticism by living American
poets. Yet Steele's argument founders on two specific points: his essentialism and his estimation of the place and role of metrical regularity.
On both points, Bernstein offers an alternative approach.

Essentialism, defined by the *Oxford Dictionary of Philosophy* as "the
doctrine that it is correct to distinguish between those properties of a

thing, or kind of thing, that are essential to it, and those that are merely accidental," appears in Steele's contention that meter is an unalterable function of a given language ("If one wants to invent a new prosody, one must invent a new language"), and in his hasty move from there to identifying meter as the essence of poetry. Contemporary poetry, he says, "often is judged exclusively with respect to its intentions or subject matter," leading to classifications of poets according to their respective causes; but in Steele's view, to classify poets as "Formalists" for having introduced meter into their work, as if doing so were analogous to adopting a cause, "confuses what is extrinsic to poetic structure with what is intrinsic to it." Against Steele's essentialism, according to which meter is essential to poetry and other features accidental, not only do I doubt that meter is essential, loving as I do too many free-verse poems and prose poems for that, but I also doubt, after the manner of Howard Nemerov's poem "Because You Asked about the Line between Prose and Poetry," that if there *were* an essence, even one whose consequences were perceptible, that essence could be articulated.

I doubt, finally, that poetry has *any* essence, to make the case for which I would mimic the analysis of the concept "game" early in Wittgenstein's *Philosophical Investigations*. Wittgenstein challenges his reader to consider "the proceedings that we call 'games,'" including board games, card games, ball games, and so on. "What is common to them all?" he asks. "Don't say: 'There *must* be something common, or they would not be called "games"'—but *look and see* whether there is anything common to all." Doing so reveals, according to Wittgenstein, not some feature common to all games but "a complicated network of similarities overlapping and criss-crossing." He calls the similarities "family resemblances" because they overlap like "the various resemblances between members of a family: build, features, colour of eyes, gait, temperament, etc." That we cannot identify a clear boundary for the concept "game" does not diminish its usefulness.

Similarly with poetry. Even limiting oneself arbitrarily to a single linguistic/cultural tradition, no single criterion picks out *Beowulf*, the prologue to *Henry V*, "Jubilate Agno," "Ode on a Grecian Urn," "The Armadillo," "Howl," and "The Colonel" as poetry, while excluding "Urn Burial," "The Jilting of Granny Weatherall," and "In the Heart of the

Heart of the Country," but that does not prevent readers from deter-
mining with fair accuracy and near-unanimity whether a literary work is
or is not poetry. The concept "game" has "blurred edges," according to
Wittgenstein, but so do the rules of tennis, which do not stipulate "how
high one throws the ball . . . , or how hard," leading Wittgenstein to the
rhetorical questions, "Is it even always an advantage to replace an
indistinct picture by a sharp one? Isn't the indistinct one often exactly
what is needed?" In the case of poetry, I think it is. We *want* to be able
to see Amy Gerstler's *Bitter Angel* or Frank Bidart's "Genesis 1–2:4" or
C. D. Wright's *Deepstep Come Shining* as poetry, even if we could not have
anticipated them on the basis of the concept of poetry we held before
encountering them. Clinging to meter as the essence of poetry would
prevent our doing so.

Steele views "virtually all" verse until the twentieth century as
organized "in the specifically and regularly ordered rhythmical units of
meter." Steele tacitly assumes that poetry with meter is intrinsically
superior to poetry without meter, a premise which is true if the stronger
claim is true, that poetry without meter is not poetry at all. But without
such essentialism, the five main points he makes in his five chapters
cannot establish his conclusion that "an art of measured speech nourishes" the qualities "most essential to human life" in "a way no other
pursuit can" and, indeed, have no logical bearing at all on that conclusion. It is interesting and even important to observe, as Steele does, that
modernist poets began to adopt prose cadences, but the observation
does not affirm the superiority of poetry over prose except by begging
the question. I do not disagree with Steele's major premises (the main
points in his five chapters), but I do not think that they establish his
conclusion. I agree, in other words, with his description of the historical facts, but not with the value judgment he takes these facts to support.

An alternative to Steele's view occurs in Charles Bernstein's *A
Poetics*. In place of Steele's attempt to identify poetry's essence,
Bernstein asserts an ongoing process: "We don't know what 'art' is or
does but we are forever finding out." Indeed, Bernstein asserts a kind
of paradoxical "negative essence" for poetry, claiming to identify it
precisely as "that which can't be contained by any set of formal qualities." On this particular point I find Bernstein's view both more

plausible and more fruitful. In poetry, as in the other arts, new works continually exceed the parameters inferred from earlier works, modifying the parameters that future works will exceed. This does not denigrate traditional metrical forms and values in English-language poetry, but it does deny them the status of essence.

The other of Steele's assertions with which I disagree is his view that meter submits to regularity as its norm. His argument in *Missing Measures* depends on this view throughout. Steele claims that "Meter involves more than merely a vague property of rhythm. As the [OED's first] definition indicates, the rhythm has a specific form. It repeats. Its patterns can be discerned and anticipated. Its principles are recognizable." He affirms the ancient Greek distinction between the "general patterns" of rhythm and the "regularly ordered" units of meter, a distinction that gives prose "rhythmical freedom" and poetry "metrical order." He specifies that, although any instance of language use can be scanned, for it to be metrical it must use "feet in repeated and recognizable linear or strophic units."

Steele *does* disclaim the singsong "ti-tumming" of metronomic verse, acknowledging that "it would be rather difficult to write a 'metronomic' line, a line, that is, of light and heavy syllables of perfectly equivalent alternating weight." But according to Steele the "necessary and happily infinite varieties of rhythmical contour" can exist only "within the norm of the conventional pentameter." Individual lines of poetry cannot themselves be perfectly regular, in other words, but the norm that they approximate is.

When Steele gives "An Explanation of Verse and Meter" in his next critical book, *All the Fun's in How You Say a Thing*, he spends much of the book explaining the "infinite varieties," citing examples of lines in which "one of the metrically unaccented syllables receives more speech stress than one of the metrically accented syllables" and identifying various forms of "metrical variation" and "rhythmical modulation." The numerous examples, though, do not persuade Steele away from the norm of regularity. He insists that "the chief sources of variation in metrical composition reside *within* the norm itself. Indeed, modulation is possible only so long as the meter [clearly identified here with the norm of regularity] is respected." I would argue that Steele's own examples show conclusively that regularity cannot stand as a norm, that we assert regularity in proportion to the *lack* of subtlety in our ears and our descriptions. The more acutely we perceive, the more variation we will hear.

To choose only one example, Steele scans line 10 of Keats's "To Autumn," "Until they think warm days will never cease," as iambic pentameter. He notes that "warm," a metrically unaccented syllable, "receives a good deal of speech stress," nearly as much as "days." But he insists that "days" has just enough stress to keep the foot an iamb instead of a spondee. His point is to establish the hermeneutic principle that readers should "assume that the poet is modulating rather than altering the meter," instead of jumping "to the conclusion that the poet has suddenly plunged into an experiment with exotic feet or rhythms." But why should we prefer that poets modulate meter rather than altering it? What is wrong with experimentation? What is wrong with exotic feet? And if modulation happens as universally as Steele so conclusively demonstrates that it does, what meaning does the purported regularity of meter retain?

Again, Charles Bernstein serves as Steele's shadow opposite. Bernstein thinks that poetry should not pursue regularity of meter but should—and does—chart "the turbulent phenomenon known as human being" by "the *nonperiodic flow* of its 'chaotic' prosody." The chaotic prosody "is not absolute but constrained. It is controllable not in its flowering but in the progression toward chaos and the regression from it." In identifying Bernstein again as a corrective to Steele, I do *not* assert a general superiority for Bernstein's view, which has its own problems and limitations. For example, he lets theory drive poetry, as in this sentence, which he emphasizes by italics and by setting it off as its own paragraph: *"The test of a poetics is the poetry and poetic thinking that results."* Even accepting that sentence as true, one might then argue that Steele's poetry comes closer than Bernstein's own to meeting the test of theory Bernstein's sentence proposes. My point is not to validate one and dismiss the other but to overhear their dialogue and learn from it.

Steele attempts to explain how it can be true that 1) there appear to be distinct metrical patterns (in most cases a knowledgeable reader who describes a line as iambic pentameter can expect that other knowledgeable readers would describe the line with the same term), when it is also true that 2) the pattern of speech stress in a given line of good poetry described as exemplifying a metrical pattern will not match the pattern of speech stress in another line of good poetry described as exemplifying the same metrical pattern. Steele seems to hold that the metrical patterns are real, that perfect regularity of metrical pattern establishes an acceptable range of variation for patterns of speech stress, and that the success of a pattern of speech stress depends on its falling within the acceptable range.

I think that there is a more plausible way to reconcile the apparently competing claims. A useful analogy comes from an unlikely source: *The Origin of Species*. Steele assumes that the metrical patterns are real. They exist independently from and have ontological priority over lines of poetry, which either fit or do not fit within a given pattern. Similarly, prior to Darwin many naturalists believed that species are real and exist independently from and have ontological priority over the varieties and the individuals that either fit or do not fit within them. What Darwin so elegantly showed is that we *construct* the concept of a species from observation of individuals, and that the manner of our construction could vary, so that whether we designate two clusters of individuals as distinct species or distinct varieties, for example, is arbitrary. Individual finches on the Galapagos vary one from another, as do the stress patterns of individual lines of poetry. Whether we label two individuals as members of the same variety, of different varieties of the same species, or of different species, is arbitrary, and the fact that biologists often agree on the classification tells us about their skill at applying customs of the discipline but does not imply that the concept "species" identifies an entity with real, extrasemiological existence. Similarly with poetry, our ability to group two lines with different sound patterns as examples of iambic pentameter does not imply that the metrical pattern designates some "real" entity. In nature, every individual is unique, and its success does not depend on the degree to which it approximates a pregiven concept of its species. Similarly, in poetry the stress pattern in every line is unique, and its success does not depend on its degree of approximation to a pregiven metrical pattern.

On what, then, does the success of a line of poetry depend? A wide variety of factors, of course, but in relation to meter, a line's success depends not on its confining itself to parameters set by regularity but on its negotiating between regularity and irregularity. In *Difference and Repetition*, Gilles Deleuze makes a distinction that serves well here. "The study of rhythm," he says, "allows us immediately to distinguish two kinds of repetition," cadence-repetition, which is "a regular division of time, an isochronic recurrence of identical elements," and rhythm-repetition, in which "the unequal is the most positive element," and "the reprise of points of inequality, of inflections or of rhythmic events, is more profound than the reproduction of ordinary homogeneous elements." In poetry, even "formal" poetry, it is not the "isochronic recurrence of identical elements" that creates the beauty of the lines, and the failures of isochronism that need to be explained away; it is the "inflections," the "rhythmic events," that lend beauty, and that theory should aim to comprehend.

We sometimes speak as if metrical verse and free verse were hostile countries that share a border, as if one could walk a hundred miles and stay in one country, and then with one step—a step watched by armed militia—cross into the other. But there is no border to be guarded. *All* poetry, whether "formal" or "free verse," operates between the poles of regularity and irregularity. A poem can be close enough to regularity to be (rightly) labeled "metrical" or close enough to irregularity to be (rightly) labeled "free verse," but it is not the case that metrical verse is "really" regular with a few irregularities to be explained away, or that free verse is "really" irregular with a little regularity that has slipped in.

Fixity of meter, like justice, serves as a valid and useful regulative ideal *only* when it is tempered by a contrary quality. Shylock needs Portia. A poetic line pursues, or should pursue, the aim not of being metrical, if by that term regularity is implied, but of being melodic. As the poles of excess and deficiency in Aristotelian ethics help to reveal the mean, though neither excess nor deficiency is itself a standard to be pursued, so the poles of regularity and irregularity in meter, neither of which is itself to be pursued in poetry, serve the creation of melody. An ethical mean may be nearer the excess, as courage is nearer the excess (foolhardiness) than the deficiency (timidity), and so may a line of verse be nearer to regularity of meter, as is Shakespeare's line cited by Steele, "These violent delights have violent ends," in spite of its one elided and one non-elided "violent." Similarly, a mean may be nearer the deficiency, as temperance is nearer self-denial than self-indulgence, and so may a line of verse be nearer to irregularity, as is Walt Whitman's "Lover divine and perfect Comrade." In both cases, though, the lines are melodious precisely because they make use of regularity *and* irregularity. Melody operates on analogy with Heraclitean palintropic harmony: as "there would be no harmony without high and low notes," and indeed "all things come to pass in accordance with conflict," so in poetry the melody of a line results not from regularity or irregularity but from the tension between the two.

Poetics

In a comment that does not even refer explicitly to poetry, in a book concerned primarily with linguistics and psychology rather than aesthetics, Ludwig Wittgenstein succinctly formulates the basic aesthetic question regarding poetry and also expresses the perpetual fascination with poetry that gives the question its force: "Can anything be more remarkable than this, that the *rhythm* of a sentence should be important for exact understanding of it?"

Poetics, the attempt to understand, appreciate, explain, and evaluate poetry, asks many questions: What *is* poetry? What distinguishes poetry from prose? What makes some poetry more beautiful than other poetry? What does poetry *do*? What social and political value does poetry have? Does poetry convey truth? And so on. All those questions, though, bear some relation to the question of why the rhythm of a sentence (or more narrowly the sounds of words, or more broadly the poetic elements in an utterance) matters to its meaning.

The first substantial statement of a poetics in traditional Western literature comes from Plato, who in several dialogues, especially the *Ion* and *Republic*, puts into Socrates' mouth negative evaluations of poetry. Many later commentators have tried to construe Plato's view of poetry as less condemnatory than it appears, on the assumption that no well-intentioned lover of wisdom can reject poetry, least of all Plato, whose writings are themselves so poetic. With or without mitigation, though,

Plato's condemnation of poetry exposes the centrality of the Wittgensteinian question about the importance of the rhythm of a sentence. Plato's poetics centers on the question of poetry's social and political value. He answers the question by excluding poetry from his ideal republic, but he justifies that exclusion on the basis of his answer to a different question, the one about what poetry does: poetry, he says, destroys the rational part of the soul. In turn, that answer depends on his answer to the question about what poetry *is*: Plato sees it as mimesis, a copying that substitutes a mendacious appearance for a veracious reality. But how does poetry fool its hearers into accepting the postiche? Plato says that the rhythm of a sentence seduces the *thumos*, the basest part of the soul and the adversary of reason: it "awakens and nourishes this part of the soul, and by strengthening it impairs the reason." Poetry intoxicates, Plato charges, and its musical elements are the inebriants.

Aristotle does not deny Plato's contention that poetry intoxicates, but he does assert, against Plato, that the intoxication has healthful effects. At least as tragedy, the one type of poetry for which we have extant Aristotle's full exposition, poetry does stimulate irrational states of the soul (pity and fear), but rather than strengthening their grip on the soul, as Plato believes, poetry releases us from their domination by purging us of them. Because Aristotle disagrees with Plato about what poetry does, he also disagrees about poetry's social and political value, but those two questions, central to Plato's poetics, are secondary in Aristotle's, where the accent falls heavily on clarifying what poetry is.

Following his usual method of investigation, Aristotle first identifies the genus into which poetry fits. Like Plato, Aristotle considers all poetry a mode of imitation, but unlike Plato, who sees imitation as necessarily meretricious, Aristotle considers imitation a healthy part of human nature. We delight actively in imitating, and passively in works produced by imitation; the *Nicomachean Ethics* even makes imitation one of the ways we acquire virtue. After identifying the genus of poetry, Aristotle distinguishes its species: epic, tragedy, comedy, dithyrambic and nomic poetry, and even flute- and lyre-playing. These species, he notes, differ from one another in their means (the particular combination of rhythm, language, and harmony employed), their objects (what kind of characters they portray), and their manner of imitation (narrative, dramatic, or mixed form).

Aristotle finds in tragedy six formative elements: spectacle, character, plot, diction, melody, and thought. Identifying these elements enables Aristotle to offer more subtle answers than those Plato gives to the various aesthetic questions about poetry. For instance, to the question of what distinguishes poetry from prose, Aristotle specifically discounts the easiest answer: that poetry employs verse. Putting the work of Herodotus into verse, says Aristotle, would not make it poetry. Instead, poetry differs from prose in the nature of its plot. The historian, Aristotle's exemplar of prose-writing, narrates what has happened, but the poet narrates "what may happen—what is possible according to the law of probability or necessity."

Enumeration of poetry's elements grounds not only Aristotle's answers to descriptive questions such as what distinguishes poetry from prose but also his answers to normative questions. The same thing that makes poetry *different from* prose also makes it *better than* prose: according to Aristotle, narrating what might be instead of what has been makes poetry's statements universals, unlike the merely singular statements of prose. The historian records, but the poet exemplifies. Pericles was Pericles, but Oedipus is all of us. The elements disclose what makes some poetry better than other poetry. All tragedies produce pity and fear, but one that does so primarily by use of spectacle is inferior to one that does so through its plot. The plot of a good play would arouse pity and fear simply by being told, even without the events being shown; to arouse pity and fear "by the mere spectacle is a less artistic method." Similarly, characters should be good, appropriate, realistic, and consistent; *ceteris paribus*, a poem with inconsistent characters is weaker than a poem with consistent characters.

Under the influence of Christianity, poetics in and around Europe took as its primary object the biblical texts. No figure better represents this practice than Augustine, who says Scripture does what Aristotle says tragedy does: it removes the soul's flaws. But the mechanism Augustine posits differs from Aristotle's. Tragedy, according to Aristotle, cures by catharsis, purging the offending states, pity and fear; Scripture, according to Augustine, cures by displacement, substituting the love of God for the offending state, sin. Whatever the character of its tropes (the poetic elements with which Augustine is preoccupied), a scriptural passage always signifies the love of God. Whoever "thinks that he understands the divine Scriptures or any part of them so that it does not build the double love of God and our neighbor does not understand it at all. Whoever finds a lesson there useful to the building of charity, even though he has not said what the author may be shown to have intended in that place, has not been deceived, nor is he lying in any way."

In spite of (or because of) Christianity, Aristotle's *Poetics* remained for centuries the definitive anatomy of those poetic elements for which the rhythm of a sentence stands as synecdoche in Wittgenstein's remark, as can be seen by the Aristotelian influence on figures as disparate as Thomas Aquinas and Alexander Pope. Still, the esteem accorded Aristotle's *descriptions* could not forever prevent others from questioning his *evaluations*, as the British Romantic poets did at the beginning of the nineteenth century. In his Preface to the *Lyrical Ballads*, William Wordsworth contradicts Aristotle on many points. For instance, one part of Aristotle's answer to what makes one poem better than another has to do with the element of character: in his view, tragedy is better than comedy in part because it depicts "persons who are above the common level," or, to use Northrop Frye's later neo-Aristotelian terminology, because it is written in the "high mimetic" mode. To purge us of pity and fear, says Aristotle, a poem needs to depict an unusually good person enduring unusually bad circumstances. In contrast, Wordsworth advocates what Frye would call "low mimetic" poetry, preferring to portray persons who are *on* the common level, not above it. He depicts "humble and rustic life" in the *Lyrical Ballads* "because, in that condition, the essential passions of the heart find a better soil in which they can attain their maturity, are less under restraint, and speak a plainer and more emphatic language." Could they agree for the sake of argument on Horace's observation that poetry serves a dual function—to delight and to teach—Aristotle and Wordsworth might go on to agree that poetry instructs through the example of its characters; but they would still disagree about what kinds of characters provide the best exemplars. Aristotle asks for kings, the men most nearly gods; Wordsworth wants carls, those nearest nature: "such men hourly communicate with the best objects from which the best part of language is originally derived."

Wordsworth shares Aristotle's disdain for spectacle, asserting the inferiority not only of spectacular poems but even of people who demand spectacle: "one being is elevated above another, in proportion as he possesses" the capability "of being excited without the application of gross and violent stimulants." But Wordsworth disagrees with the primacy Aristotle grants to plot. Wordsworth answers the question of what poetry is by calling it "the spontaneous overflow of powerful feelings." By making feeling definitive of poetry, he also gives it precedence over plot: "the feeling therein developed gives importance to the action and situation, and not the action and situation to the feeling."

In Wordsworth, as in Plato and Aristotle, the foregrounded question betrays its immediate connection to the Wittgensteinian question about the importance of the musical elements to understanding. The poet's extraordinary capacity for feeling leads poetry "to produce excitement in co-existence with an overbalance of pleasure." Wordsworth thus agrees with Plato that poetry produces "an unusual and irregular state of the mind; ideas and feelings do not, in that state, succeed each other in accustomed order." But the rhythm of the sentence alleviates the danger of this overstimulated state of mind: "the co-presence of something regular," namely the meter of the poem, "cannot but have great efficacy in tempering and restraining the passion."

Less than a quarter-century after Wordsworth in his Preface disputed Aristotle's views on plot and character, Percy Bysshe Shelley in *A Defence of Poetry* seconded Aristotle's asseverations of poetry's truth against Plato's accusations of its falsity. "A poem," Shelley says, "is the image of life expressed in its eternal truth." As with other theorists, Shelley's answer to the question that preoccupies him (whether poetry conveys truth) connects with his answers to the other questions of poetics, in particular the question about the importance of the rhythm of a sentence. Like Aristotle, Shelley refuses as oversimplified the most obvious answer to the question about what distinguishes poetry from prose. Shelley contends that "the popular division into prose and verse is inadmissible in accurate philosophy" and should be replaced by "the distinction between measured and unmeasured language." Doing so, he claims, would clarify that the rhythm of a sentence invokes truth.

Unlike Aristotle, who asserts only a greater *potential* for truth in the universal statements of poetry than in the singular statements of prose, Shelley insists on the necessity of truth in poetry. For Aristotle, poetry's truth-telling is a matter of degree: a poem is capable of more truth than is prose, and presumably capable of more falsehood as well. But for Shelley, poetry's truth is absolute: if it is poetry, it tells the truth. "All the authors of revolutions in opinion" are necessarily poets partly because they are inventors whose "words unveil the permanent analogy of things by images which participate in the life of truth," but mostly because "their periods are harmonious and rhythmical, and contain in themselves the elements of verse; being the echo of the eternal music."

The question about the relation of sound and sense remains central in contemporary poetics, informing its various preoccupations. For example, both the philosopher Hans-Georg Gadamer and the poet Louise Glück cite "the rhythm of a sentence" in their own answers to the question of whether poetry conveys truth.

That the relation between sound and meaning stands as the crux of poetry's truthfulness appears in Gadamer's writing when he announces that he considers "incontrovertible" the "particular and unique relationship to truth" enjoyed by what he names not poetry but, more specifically, "poetic language." Gadamer argues for poetry's truth-telling character by a genus-and-species definition. Poetry belongs to the genus of "autonomous" texts, along with two other species, religious texts and legal texts. The religious text is a pledge, which can be called on and relied on as binding in ways that mere communication cannot, but only when "acknowledged on the part of the believer." The legal text, too, is binding, but becomes so only by declaration and promulgation throughout a community.

Poetry belongs in the category of autonomous texts because, like religious and legal texts, it claims completeness. It "expresses fully what the given state of affairs is." Poetry's specific difference from religious and legal texts, though, lies in its being "self-fulfilling." Religious and legal texts effect their aims only through the complicity of their audience, but poetry "bears witness to itself and does not admit anything that might verify it." Gadamer illustrates his point by appeal to the staircase down which Smerdjakov falls in *The Brothers Karamazov*. Every reader knows exactly—and correctly—what the staircase looks like, even though Dostoevsky himself could not adjudicate an argument between a reader who contends the staircase turns to the right and one who contends it turns to the left. The poet, Gadamer says, "manages to conjure up the self-fulfillment of language." Poetry resembles less an assertion of empirical fact than a performative utterance. It *does* something, and the doing subjects it to coherence rather than correspondence as the criterion for its truth.

But *how* does poetry assume this disposition? The answer should by now be predictable: "in the language of poetry, the dimensions of sound and sense are inextricably interwoven." Because of the sound of its words, the rhythm of its sentences, "the poetic creation does not intend something, but rather is the existence of what it intends." Sound and rhythm, Gadamer says, raise the poem above the need for confirmation by the world, giving it a necessary rather than a contingent connection to truth. A poem is no more subject to empirical validation or invalidation than is a symphony. Or, to use a sentence from Wittgenstein as another avatar of Gadamer's idea: "Do not forget that a poem, even though it is composed in the language of information, is not used in the language game of giving information."

The question of whether poetry conveys truth Gadamer answers in one way, by an answer to the question of what poetry is; Louise Glück answers the same question in a different way, by an answer to what makes one poem better than another. Glück argues that an artist's success "depends on conscious willingness to distinguish truth from honesty or sincerity." Our customary association of honesty with truth Glück calls "a form of anxiety." She defines truth as "the embodied vision, illumination, or enduring discovery which is the ideal of art."

Glück argues that honest speech is merely a relief, but true speech is a discovery. Like Gadamer, she subjects poetry to a coherence rather than a correspondence standard of truth: "Any attempt to evaluate the honesty of a text must always lead away from that text, and toward intention," but any attempt to evaluate the truth of a text leads into the text, and it does so via the rhythm of the sentences. When Glück sets out to elucidate the truth of her three illustrative works, poems by John Keats, John Milton, and John Berryman, she does so by studying the musical elements of the poems. She connects truth to "distinctive voice," itself inseparable from rhythm. An informed reader can recognize the voice of Keats in the rhythm of his poems no less certainly than one recognizes the voice of a friend or lover by its rhythms. Truth, in Glück's view, is elemental, incapable of change in form without change in substance, and its elemental character derives from and is manifested in the musical elements of the poem.

Like Gadamer's and Glück's accounts of poetry's truth, recent attempts to answer other questions in poetics touch on the relation of sound and sense. The last quarter of the twentieth century saw heated debates over what should be included in the poetic canon (one form of the question of what makes one poem better than another). Albert Cook's entry in that debate argues that the criterion for including a poem or body of poetry in the canon should be its wisdom. Wise poetry should be included, unwise poetry excluded. Cook states explicitly his intention not to consider rhythm. "Wisdom," he says, "comes about through a strategic combination of features," namely thought, image, and story. Cook alludes to Ezra Pound's list of relevant features, melopoeia (charging the words "with some musical property" that directs the "bearing" of their meaning), phanopoeia (imagery), and logopoeia ("the dance of the intellect among words"), but what Pound placed first—rhythm—Cook eliminates.

Or tries to eliminate. Cook makes wisdom his criterion for canon formation, but rhythm proves to be a component of wisdom. Explaining why *Leaves of Grass* should be canonized, but *Hiawatha* should not, Cook calls Whitman's wisdom "far more complex" than Longfellow's and attributes that complexity in large part to "the rhythms of *Leaves of Grass*." Not all wisdom is complex, though: some resides "in a radiant simplicity." Still, Cook argues for the generality of the connection between poetry's musical elements and its wisdom, contending that *any* explication of the superiority of one poem's wisdom to that of another poem will appeal to "the particular arrangement of language that brings about so penetrating an utterance."

Even in the apparently paradoxical preoccupation with silence in recent poetics, the Wittgensteinian question about the relation of sound and sense has a place. No ingredient appears more frequently in recent *ars poetica* poems than silence. Archibald MacLeish's "Ars Poetica" avers that a poem should be

mute
As a globed fruit,

Dumb
As old medallions to the thumb,

Silent as the sleeve-worn stone
Of casement ledges where the moss has grown —

A poem should be wordless
As the flight of birds.

Heather McHugh begins her volume of selected poems with "What He Thought," a poem in which one of the characters recounts the execution of Giordano Bruno on charges of heresy. Fearing his eloquence, "his captors / placed upon his face / an iron mask," in which they burned him. "That is how / he died," the speaker says, "without a word, in front / of everyone. // And poetry . . . is what // he thought, but did not say." W. S. Merwin describes poetry as "what passes between // us now in a silence / on this side of the flames."

The relation between the silence so often alluded to by poets and "the rhythm of a sentence" receives its explicit formulation in T. S. Eliot's "Four Quartets." After saying that "Words, after speech, reach / Into the silence," Eliot explains *how*: "Only by the form, the pattern, / Can words or music reach / The stillness." Poets' frequent recourse to silence in their own poetics expresses the fact that a poem cannot be reduced to its propositional content, as if (returning now to Wittgenstein) to modify the Tractarian maxim that "What can be shown, cannot be said," not by reducing language to pictures but by insisting that neither sound nor sense can be separated from the totality that is the poem. The sense of a poem cannot be *ex*tracted because the form cannot be *sub*tracted. In Eliot's formulation: "the sound of a poem is as much an abstraction from the poem as is the sense."

Silence has become a stock poetic metaphor for the inseparability of sound and sense, the untranslatability of poetry, the inevitability of the poem that prevents it from being restated. Sound and sense generate a totality greater than its parts, and that totality prohibits adding anything to the poem by further speech. Thus contemporary poets make a virtue of the vice Socrates in the *Phaedrus* attributes to writing: writing fails, he says, because, unlike speech, it cannot defend itself from misinterpretation and will not respond when queried. It speaks once, but cannot speak again. Poetry, like Giordano Bruno in Heather McHugh's poem, refuses to defend itself. The frequent appeal to silence in the statements of poetics offered by recent poets means not that poems do not speak, but that they do not speak twice.

To assert the centrality to any poetics of the question why the rhythm of a sentence should be important for understanding is not to accept the doctrine of formalism, a particular poetics with its roots in Kant and its flowering in critics like Eliot and Cleanth Brooks, but to acknowledge that any question about poetry will include within itself a question about form. "The rhythm of a sentence," the formal aspects of a poem, will not be the exclusive focus of any attempt to understand poetry, but will be a part of every attempt.

Abstraction's Command

When the narrator in W. S. Merwin's "The River of Bees" says with evident sarcasm that "Men think they are better than grass," he takes issue with a long tradition in Western intellectual history of hierarchizing natural forms. Whether manifest as Heraclitus' contention that "the most beautiful of apes is ugly in comparison to the race of men, the wisest of men seems an ape in comparison to a god," or as Descartes's argument that animals not only "have less reason than men, but that they have none at all," or even as the hostile early response to Darwin's theory, the long-standard view has placed humans above the rest of nature. Merwin's dispute with the traditional view extends beyond "The River of Bees" to play an important role in a sizable portion of his work.

Merwin's corpus to date divides itself easily into three periods: an early period that runs through the first four books and ends abruptly at *The Moving Target*, with its use of "open form" in place of traditional metrical and stanzaic forms; a middle, oracular period that ends with *The Compass Flower*; and a late period of more transparently personal and intimate poetry, foretold by the anomalous *Finding the Islands* and then begun in earnest with the family poems in *Opening the Hand*.

Among its other distinctive features, the middle period emphasizes animism and primitivism. Merwin regularly treats inanimate objects (stones, crosses, dust, and so on) as if they were animate and treats ani-

mals as if they were human. Within that broad pattern, a more particular pattern leads to a kind of poem, the poem of abstraction's command,
that can be read as the quintessence of Merwin's middle period. The
more particular pattern is a thematic continuum that funnels from
apostrophizing animals to apostrophizing abstraction(s) and culminates in reverse apostrophe when the abstraction addresses us.

In his early and late periods, Merwin shows no less interest in animals than in his middle period, but he maintains a different stance
toward them. In the early and late periods, the distinction between
humans and other animals remains intact, in the manner of Auden's
"Their Lonely Betters": "As I listened from a beach-chair in the shade /
To all the noises that my garden made, / It seemed to me only proper
that words / Should be withheld from vegetables and birds."

In "Herons," for example, which takes its place in *A Mask for Janus*
as the first poem in Merwin's collected work with the name of an animal in its title, the three herons—reminiscent of the three women in
Yeats's "Friends"—seem to speak, but they do so only in a dream, the
human narrator's dream, where their words clearly represent the
words of the narrator or his unconscious. The herons have voice only
insofar as they have been transported by the dream from their world
into the narrator's. Similarly, in *The Dancing Bears*, the heron in "The
Lady with the Heron" serves only as a correlative for the lady. The narrator's interest in the heron depends wholly on his interest in the lady,
and he attributes to the heron no character or identity except as a figure for the lady.

Merwin's preoccupation with animals becomes the focal point of
Green with Beasts, as the book's title indicates, but even so, only the
human voice has the authority to speak of and to the animals. The book's
first part, "Physiologus: Chapters for a Bestiary," consists of a series in
which each poem describes some animal or pair of animals. In each
case, a human voice speaks about the animal from a point of view outside—and above—it. "This is the black sea-brute bulling through wave-
wrack," the human narrator of the first poem, "Leviathan," begins. The
narrator in "Blue Cockerel" looks at "this bird" balancing, "His blue
feet splayed." "White Goat, White Ram" gives a premonition of the
coming change in point of view when the speaker recognizes as ironic
the fact that "out of our dumbness / We would speak for them, give

speech to the mute tongues / Of angels," but the animals still remain a "them" apart from "us" throughout *Green with Beasts*, including the animal poems scattered through the rest of the book: "Burning the Cat," "Dog Dreaming," "A Sparrow Sheltering under a Column of the British Museum," and others. The same stance defines the (far less frequent) animal poems in *The Drunk in the Furnace*, poems such as "Some Winter Sparrows."

In *The Moving Target*, though, the formal transition away from metrical forms and punctuation signals changes in voice, point of view, and theme, none more significant than the new way in which animals assert themselves in the poems. As early as the book's third poem, "Lemuel's Blessing," animals become subjects instead of objects. Though the poem begins with a human voice blessing a wolf distinct from itself ("I bless your paws and their twenty nails which tell their own prayer"), soon the identification with the wolf becomes so thorough that the subject and object merge. From a wish ("Let me wear the opprobrium of possessed and possessors / As a thick tail . . .") the identification becomes a fact ("Deliver me / . . . From the ruth of known paths, which would use my feet, tail, and ears as curios"). That identification paves the way for poems like "Noah's Raven," in which the animal in the poem speaks for itself.

The shift from being spoken about to speaking or being spoken through may seem only a slight change in accent, but it amounts to a recognition about subject/object relations like the one William H. Gass articulates about the relation between the terms in metaphor: "We are inclined to think that in metaphors only one term is figurative," when in fact "the terms are inspecting one another—they interact—the figure is drawn both ways." In "Some Winter Sparrows," which begins "I hear you already, choir of small wheels," one term, the subject, inspects the other, the object, and the reverse inspection can happen only covertly. The subject/object relations change, though, as soon as Merwin's middle period begins. In "Noah's Raven," which begins "Why should I have returned?," the speaker and the bird have become one, so that both forms of inspection, of object by subject and of subject by object, are overt and equivalent.

The identification of speaker and animal does not continue into *The Lice*, but the mutual inspection of subject and object does. If in "Some

Winter Sparrows" the narrator seems conscious only of his scrutinizing the birds, assuming that they are oblivious to him, in "The Animals," which opens *The Lice*, the narrator explicitly recognizes the mutual scrutiny. The initial image of "blind crosses sweeping the tables"— the shadows of window frames moving across tables as the sun moves—is paralleled by "myself tracking over empty ground" in a way that establishes a ratio. The crosses are blind in spite of being made by sunlight, the speaker "never saw" the animals in spite of his sharing their ancestry. The ratio is overdetermined: I am to the blind crosses as the animals are to light, but also I am to the animals as the blind crosses are to light. The speaker remains the speaker, but—paradoxically—he is mute and the animals have voice. The speaker's Adamic responsibility for naming the animals still haunts him, but he cannot fulfill it: "I with no voice // Remembering names to invent for them." The Audenian roles have been reversed: instead of being "withheld from vegetables and birds" and given to humans, words are withheld from humans but given to vegetables and birds.

That role reversal, in which animals speak, constitutes one shift along the thematic continuum. It enables the poems to give voice to human obligation as imperatives derived from external sources; it sets up the animals as external correlatives to obligations felt as internal experiences, a gesture that culminates in the sequence of poems, late in *The Lice*, from "For a Coming Extinction" through "Fly." There, animals teach the speaker about his responsibilities. In "For a Coming Extinction" the responsibility is collective: "we" humans, not any "I" alone, "are sending you to The End // That great god." The irony of human failure of collective responsibility toward an entire species receives emphasis from the ambiguity of number in the nouns and pronouns of address: although one assumes the speaker addresses the Gray Whale as a species, "gray whale" and "you" could be read in each case as addressing an individual whale. Like whales' songs to each other, responsibilities echo back and forth between the speaker and the whales: the speaker's allusion to the religious doctrine that God created humans in a separate act from his creation of animals, "Tell him that we were made / On another day," stated as a request to the whale, functions ironically because the speaker's awareness of the human threat to the whale species' existence puts the lie to the likeness between humans and God that the doctrine alleges.

In "Avoiding News by the River," the distinction between humans and animals is not that words are withheld from one but not the other, but that only humans experience shame, with the implicit corollary that only humans *should*. The poem ends: "If I were not human I would not be ashamed of anything." That shame culminates in "Fly," where only the death of the animal, in this case "a fat pigeon," can reveal to the human his own identity ("I found him in the dovecote dead / Of the needless efforts // So that is what I am") and his tragic flaw, ironically the very Audenian difference these poems reverse: believing "too much in words."

Animals continue to speak through Merwin's middle books, in poems such as "The Owl" and "Words from a Totem Animal" in *The Carrier of Ladders* and "A Flea's Carrying Words" in *Writings to an Unfinished Accompaniment*. But *Writings* also contains two related poems located nearby on the same thematic continuum. "Animals from Mountains" presents itself as a record of the inner experience of identification and communion with animals. The speaker recalls that "When I was small and stayed quiet / some animals came," and "they knew me." No one else saw them, but "they waited right there" and then "we went out one time / onto one mountain" and "the next day the mountain was gone." The trips onto mountains continue, but the poem concludes that "some of us / never came back all the way." "The Track" focuses on the consequences of the speaker's identification with animals:

> To see that an ancestor has reappeared
> as the print of a paw
> in a worn brick
> changes what you believe you are
> and where you imagine you are going

The adoption of a perspective from which animals can speak leads Merwin to another shading in the thematic continuum: inanimate objects, too, speak, in the same literal and figurative ways that animals do. On the page following "Lemuel's Blessing" early in *The Moving*

Target, Merwin continues his dizzying "descent" through Aristotle's souls, from rational through animal and vegetable, on his way to ensouling the unsouled. That one page contains "In the Gorge," in which trees speak, describing themselves as "grop[ing] for each other" across the stream, then asking the "Lord of the bow" their despairing question "Have you left us nothing but your blindness?" It also contains "By Day and By Night," in which the human speaker addresses the shadow, praising it as if it could hear and asking it questions as if expecting an answer. The movement through Aristotle's souls feels like a descent because we so commonly apply, without reflection or even conscious awareness, the principle that our responsibility toward something depends on its likeness to ourselves (as in the argument by animal rights advocates that animals' rights resemble ours because the animals resemble us, especially in being sensate). Merwin's practice in these poems, though, approximates the Hegelian ideal: "To consider a thing rationally means not to bring reason to bear on the object from the outside and so to tamper with it, but to find that the object is rational on its own account."

The epitome of the poems that speak to and through inanimate objects is "Things." In that poem, the "things" address their "possessor," naming their virtues in the first stanza: "Better than friends, in your sorrows we take no pleasure," they say, and "We are the anchor of your future." In the second stanza, they make promises to "be all the points on your compass" and to "give you interest on yourself as you deposit yourself with us," and impose a concluding request: "Be a gentleman: you acquired us when you needed us, / We do what we can to please, we have some beauty, we are helpless, / Depend on us." Merwin's things talking about themselves to a human assume a point of view similar to the one expressed by a human talking about things in Nietzsche's *The Gay Science*.

> Avarice and love: what different feelings these two terms evoke! Nevertheless it could be the same instinct that has two names— once deprecated by those who *have*, in whom the instinct has calmed down to some extent, and who are afraid for their "possessions," and the other time seen from the point of view

of those who are not satisfied but still thirsty and who therefore glorify the instinct as "good." . . . Our pleasure in ourselves tries to maintain itself by again and again changing something new *into ourselves*; that is what possession means. To become tired of some possession means tiring of ourselves.

In "Things," and in poems like "Inscription for a Burned Bridge," Merwin takes Rilke's advice: ". . . if there is nothing in common between you and other people, try being close to things, they will not desert you."

The thematic continuum that gives voice to animals and to inanimate objects culminates in poems in which abstractions, rather than things, speak or are spoken to. "For the Grave of Posterity," also in *The Moving Target*, exemplifies this approach. A human speaker first describes a gravestone and then gives way to it, but the stone is an abstraction, a stone "that is / not here and bears no writing" yet still "commemorates / the emptiness at the end of / history." And the stone that is not here speaks of "nothing it is the voice with the praises / that never changed," which itself "called to the unsatisfied." The names of things continue to appear in this poem, but only as abstractions from the things themselves, described primarily by negation. Other poems in which abstractions speak or are spoken to include "The Last One," "My Brothers the Silent," "Encounter," "The Free," and "Provision," which concludes: "I will take you with me the emptiness of my hands / What you do not have you find everywhere."

That the abstractions receive primarily apophatic description— "Something I've Not Done," "The Unwritten"—allies them with that apotheosis of abstractions, God, so often described by the faithful in the terms of negative theology, and by others as guilty of the charge with which Merwin's "Before That" begins: "It was never there and already it's vanishing." Such an alliance makes it predictable that not long after the abstractions begin to speak, they will begin to give commands, and the thematic continuum I am describing culminates in poems that serve as the tables of the abstractions' law.

Again the important sequence of short poems at the beginning of *The Moving Target* provides a first example of this kind of poem in "Dead

Hand," whose disembodied speaker ends his short statement with the imperative to "Hang it up till the rings fall." The pattern receives further development in *The Lice* in "A Scale in May," where an ambiguous speaker (the "I"? the five poplars?) orders: "To succeed consider what is as though it were past / Deem yourself inevitable and take credit for it / If you find you no longer believe enlarge the temple."

The poems of abstraction's command culminate in "Exercise," "Instructions to Four Walls," and "Ballade of Saying," all three within a few pages of each other in *Writings to an Unfinished Accompaniment*. "Exercise" offers no context or explanation for its opening imperative: "First forget what time it is / for an hour / do it regularly every day." Not the voice of divine command speaking to Moses from the burning bush or to Job from the whirlwind, this wholly disembodied voice speaks from nowhere, to no one, and apropos of nothing. Each command exceeds the one before it in the scope of its erasure, a Cartesian *Discourse* without the saving, indubitable "I." The auditor of the poem is ordered to "forget how to count / starting with your own age / starting with how to count backward," and arriving through a series of such steps at a state in which "everything is continuous again." But the commands become even more broad and basic in their scope: "go on to forgetting elements / starting with water / proceeding to earth / rising in fire // forget fire."

Although Merwin most often hears abstraction command in verse, his prose from the middle period sometimes works within the same thematic continuum, as exemplified most vividly by "Make This Simple Test," which, published in *The Miner's Pale Children*, anticipates by three years its sister poem, "Exercise." "Make This Simple Test" begins with the injunction to "Blindfold yourself with some suitable object," and then describes a process for taste-testing to see whether the subject can identify the contents of a food product by taste. But as in "Exercise," each command in the series becomes more ambitious (and abstract), with no apparent regard for the limits of possibility:

> Guess again what you are eating or drinking in each case (if you can make the distinction). But this time do not stop there. Guess why you are eating or drinking it. Guess what it may do

for you. Guess what it was meant to do for you. . . . Guess at the taste of locusts and wild honey. Guess at the taste of water. Guess what the rivers see as they die. Guess why the babies are burning. Guess why there is silence in heaven. Guess why you were ever born.

If "Make This Simple Test" is the closest kin of "Exercise," "Instructions to Four Walls" is its closest neighbor. "Instructions" alters the direction of command from that in "Exercise," but to similar effect. Though the speaker (a human) and the audience (four walls) receive more particular specification than in "Exercise," the peculiar relation between the two (dis)orients the reader in a manner similar to the lack of context in "Exercise." By addressing the four walls, the speaker leads the reader to identify with the walls, and the unlikeness between a human and a wall gives the commands the same feeling of inexplicability that the commands in "Exercise" exercise. "Now one of you turn this way / just as you are," the narrator orders, "speaking another language / as the earth does / and open your eyes / with the wall inside them / doubled." As in "Exercise," the commands culminate in impossibilities:

> and one of you
> stay still just as you are
> with your door
> be yesterday
> be tomorrow
> be today

In "Ballade of Sayings," the continuum arrives at its terminus. The commands of abstraction, with only one exception ("you kill the front of him I'll kill the back"), must be themselves abstracted from the proverbs presented as statements of fact. "Nowhere are the martyrs more beautiful," the poem says, and "the poor do not exist they are just the poor." Thus Merwin completes the return to the "normal" poetic methodology of a poem such as "Choice of Prides" from *The Drunk in the Furnace*, but after experience and therefore to wholly different effect.

83

Now the speaker's voice carries a different authority, that of the zoologist who has lived with the apes for a decade or the god who has seen other wars. There will still follow failures such as *The Compass Flower*, but from the middle period on, even when the voice in a Merwin poem speaks very particularly *sub specie humanitatem*, as in the family poems in *Opening the Hand* or the poems of France in *The Vixen*, it will have the timbre that comes from having seen *sub specie aeternitatem*.

Gently Omitting

A ny river has eddies and wash at its edges where water pauses or pools away from the current.

Laura Riding's *Though Gently* calls on—and calls to—an acroamatic, heteroclite tradition. Not Plato and Aristotle, Augustine and Descartes, Kant and Hegel, Heidegger and Derrida, the tradition of dialogue and discourse that thinks that the longer we talk the more we know, the tradition of Homer and Dante and Wordsworth and Pound that tries to account for the world by accumulation, the tradition of rudely including. *Though Gently* beckons instead the tradition of "gently omitting," of Heraclitus and Lao Tzu and the Christian mystics and Simone Weil, the tradition of those for whom the less said, the better, the skoteinographic tradition that expects words to resonate in darkness but not to illuminate.

Disaster need not offer a moral. The migrating bird burdened by ice in early cold, fallen from its flight path. Sometimes one should *not* learn.

Some of *Though Gently*'s sisters: Auden, *The Prolific and the Devourer*; Blake, *The Marriage of Heaven and Hell*; Canetti, *The Human Province*;

Ekelund, *The Second Light*; Fowles, *The Aristos*; Irigaray, *Elemental Passions*; Leopardi, *Pensieri*; Nietzsche, *Daybreak*; the notebooks of Oppen and Roethke; Porchia, *Voices*; Schlegel, *Philosophical Fragments*; Stevens, *Adagia*; Zwicky, *Lyric Philosophy*. Orphans all.

Some silts silhouette heads on pillows, some sediments save the shapes of skeletons in secret for centuries. The fine grain at its patient work, servant to wind and water.

WHAT IS THERE TO BELIEVE IN: The rib cage buried beside the bones of Wittgenstein's *Tractatus*, its widow, dead nine years later, her testament eight statements instead of seven, but with less muttering in between.

Can anything that is not poetry say anything about what is poetry? Can anything that is poetry ever have been anything else? A molten flow escapes through the seams where our categories slide against and fold over each other.

Rude includers want to know how much we must say before we say for certain. If the grammar of our language replicates the world, then the longer we sing, the more replete our map. But what begins with *There is a no-sense and a corresponding sense* must end with the question of the gentles: *And how much may we omit without not telling the truth?* And then stop, without expecting to know more, and without claiming to have discovered more.

Sooner listen to God tell obscurely of woman than to man tell plainly of God.

Prayer. Love. *Not for the benefit of what follows, for nothing follows.* Logic. Poetry. *Because* nothing follows. Corrupt if anything did. *Nothing follows.* A thought we cannot think, since thinking seeks what follows, but which (from what we *can* think) we know must be true. Poetry's incorrigible dishonesty: in poetry one thing *always* follows from another.

The Devil always wins the argument because only the Devil can name God without guilt. Who owes God nothing speaks freely, and the Devil pays his debts.

We speak to gods we believe in, and hear from the gods we don't.

So *that* is what poems listen for: *a consistent impossibility*. A disturbance in the magnetic field powerful enough to produce light. An unlikely return through the sea to bury your children in the same sand from which you dug yourself out. A migratory cycle no single generation completes. The chatter of playing neighborhood children decayed into song.

Feeding the songbirds. Naming strays. Rising in time to hear the owl. Measuring rainfall. *I mean to say precisely that we have stopped.*

Gentles suspend disbelief in Riding's allegation that *Thinking of one thing you cannot help thinking of everything.* Or George Oppen's: *Every object includes the universe in its constitution and the laws of its being.* Thought consists not in an Aristotelian accumulation but, like perception, which selects the smallest number of sensations from the plethora of possible percepts, in a winnowing, a narrowing down to the one thing needful. The bat echolocating a moth against a background of leaves in the breeze. A widow willing to bear the wind to hear the last leaf torn from the tree. An anorexic girl slowly ceding herself to her will to watch the world instead of consuming it.

> Look truthfully. Say nothing that can be omitted.
> Sing gently. Gently listen.

Cold Baths

The cramped cultural space poetry currently occupies puts curious parameters on poets' responsibility to review new poetry by others. The minimal space typically allowed for reviews of new poetry books forces one to adopt the mind-set recommended by Nietzsche. "I approach deep problems," he says, "like cold baths: quickly into them and quickly out again. That one does not get to the depths that way, not deep enough down, is the superstition of those afraid of the water, the enemies of cold water; they speak without experience. The freezing cold makes one swift." For inclusion here, I have chosen from reviews of established poets a few that seemed to me to express some relevant insight or to take a minority viewpoint in regard to the book in question. I follow those with a few reviews of less well-known poets for whose work I wish to advocate.

Frank Bidart and Michael Waters

Shakespeare should have stopped Sonnet 116 sooner. Love is not love. Period. Qualifications, ameliorations, and specifications constitute only a turning away, a refusal. Avoid eye contact with love, lie to it, and like a horse or a dog it will submit, will forfeit its nature to adopt yours, will become as harmless as a declawed cat or a greeting card.

But stare love down, admit it as something more grave than Meg Ryan paring an apple peel into one spiraling piece, square to it as something on which one stakes one's life: What then? A few poets in any age will ask, so Frank Bidart and Michael Waters, each of whom wants to look love or its avatars in the eye, have antecedents. In *Desire*, Bidart identifies his. Nearly every poem in the volume announces its atavism, naming such ancestors as Plotinus, Dante, Catullus, Borges, Tacitus, Marcus Aurelius, and Berlioz. Waters's consanguines are tacit and more contemporary than Bidart's, but they haunt his work nonetheless: Jack Gilbert and Louise Glück might be Waters's father and sister by age or preoccupation.

Bidart and Waters understand love's defiance of the law of identity and so share Rilke's view of love as "the most difficult of all our tasks, the ultimate, the last test and proof, the work for which all other work is but preparation." For Bidart, the difficulty of love, its refusal of self-identity, lies in the realm of possibility/necessity. For Waters, the difficulty lies in the realm of potentiality/actuality. That difference means that in Bidart love proves impossible; in Waters it proves unreal.

As a result, love in Bidart assumes (as his title indicates) the form of desire: the recognition of happiness but without the ability to attain it. Bidart's master here, though he never names him, is Hobbes, who makes this epistemological distinction: "*Appetite* with an opinion of attaining, is called Hope. The same, without such opinion, Despaire." Change the modality of Hobbes's distinction, and you get Bidart: appetite with the possibility of attaining is greed; without such possibility, love. Its impossibility makes love show itself in Bidart as paradox: "we are the wheel to which we are bound," he says in "Overheard through the Walls of the Invisible City." Similarly, he translates Catullus: "*I hate and—love.* The sleepless body hammering a nail nails / itself, hanging crucified." In the longer "Borges and I," he arrives more than once at paradox. "The notion that Frank has a self that has remained the same and that knows what it would be if its writing self did not exist—like all assertions about the systems that hold sway beneath the moon, the opposite of this seems to me to be true, as true."

Bidart arrives at paradox but also at others of impossibility's sisters: fate/destiny, nihilism, and illusion. Fate in the koan "Homo Faber":

"Whatever lies still uncarried from the abyss within / me as I die dies with me." And in the elegy "In Memory of Joe Brainard": ". . . the soul // learns once again the body it loves and hates is / made of earth, and will betray it." Illusion in "The Yoke," where the speaker evokes one lost, with "don't worry   I know you're dead / but tonight // turn your face again." And explicitly in the view of the Stoics in "The Return," where the philosophers opine on a Roman army returned to bury the dead of three legions six years after their defeat.

> When these events were reported to Rome
>
> Cynics whispered that *thus* the cunning State
> enslaves us to its failures and its fate.—
>
> Epicureans saw in the ghostly mire
> an emblem of the nature of Desire.—
>
> Stoics replied that life is War, ILLUSION
> the source, the goal, the end of human action.

Finally, nihilism in "Lady Bird": "so when we followed that golden couple into the White House // I was aware that people look at / the living, and wish for the dead." And again in "The Return," his revision of Tacitus, which ends with this couplet: "Arminius, relentlessly pursued by / Germanicus, retreated into pathless country." For Bidart, any trail followed long enough leads, like the famine roads in Eavan Boland's "That the Science of Cartography Is Limited," to pathless country.

If for Bidart the impossibility of love gives it the form of desire and entails paradox, fate, illusion, and nihilism, for Waters the unreality of love gives it the form of suggestion and entails anticipation, regret, and dream. Desire is the recognition of happiness without the ability to attain it; suggestion, the recognition of *meaning* without the ability to *create* it.

"Stoning the Birds" depicts well the anticipatory character love has for Waters, its manner of being always almost but not quite present. In this poem a young boy on a summer vacation with his family "veers off the horse trail" while hunting birds and happens upon "some couple lovemaking among the pines," after which in his bewilderment he wishes he could dive into the pool and "remain / underwater till the summer was over, / hold my breath till the planet stopped whirling // long enough for me to grasp it with cupped hands." The same anticipatory character of love appears in "Everlasting Pea": "When we touched along the flared lengths of our limbs," he writes,

> we assumed our habitation among the everlasting,
> their swollen, sensual beauty always
>
> on the verge of flight, almost
> apart from creeping leaf and tendril, almost
> another trick of the light. But that silence:
>
> that *something-about-to-happen.* . . .

The same love that stays always almost but not quite present because it has not yet arrived, stays always almost but not quite present because it has already left. So for Waters, anticipation changes easily into regret, as in "Not Love," a reminiscence of "that woman I couldn't love / long enough, and for whom, not loving, / I began to perfect these small, / sacramental gestures." Or "Avesta," in which the narrator finds a sparrow's nest that includes strands of his departed lover's red hair. As he holds it, "the nest crumbles . . . into filaments."

Inevitably, unreality becomes dream, as in "The Curiosities," in which a pair of lovers, after visiting a medical museum with its specimens preserved in formaldehyde, are haunted by "these jars stuffed with the invisible / masses who touch us in our dreams." Dream appears even more centrally in the one poem in the book where Waters replicates Bidart's manner of explicitly responding to a precedent text. Waters quotes Knut Hamsun:

'I love three things,' I say then. 'I love a dream of love I once
had, I love you, and I love this patch of earth.'
    'And which do you love best?'
    'The dream.'

Interestingly, that quotation—the one sample of words not Waters's own—comes as close as any short passage to summarizing Waters's book.

Waters's book is elegant and lyrical, a littoral studded with glistening shells. Bidart's is oracular, another proof that the gods never fall silent.

John Ashbery

Every age adores a few poets in whose work posterity maintains no interest. James Henry Leigh Hunt in his own time enjoyed much greater popularity (and better connections) than did Keats. Longfellow, Whittier, Holmes, and Lowell were much more popular than their almost exact contemporaries Whitman and Dickinson. Already the sun has set on Sandburg, MacLeish, and others of our century's passing fancies. Like sycophants who rise and fall with the political leaders they serve, such poets rise and fall with the Zeitgeist they feed. John Ashbery is such a poet, adored by the age because he says what it wants to hear, but destined for obscurity when the times change. *And the Stars Were Shining* shows why.

The first poem in the collection typifies the book as a whole. Its title, "Token Resistance," resembles many of the others in being formulaic and empty. Some are clichés ("'The Favor of a Reply"); some, the names of banal objects ("Gummed Reinforcements"); some, imitations of famous titles ("On First Listening to Schreker's *Der Schatzgräber*"); and some are common phrases ("Well, Yes, Actually"). One of the poems, "Title Search," consists exclusively of titles, although ironically it is the book's most successful poem, since at the end of a long list of titles, each as silly as those chosen for use in the book, comes an abrupt change of tone with the simple title, "The Father," to which there is a possibility of the emotional or intellectual connection that all the other titles—in the poem and in the book—attempt to avoid. Ashbery tries to make the title a distinctive element of his style (as it is in Stevens, for instance), but by falling into formulae he only makes it a *flaw* of his style.

The cliché in the title of the first poem, repeated in the poem itself, is matched by another when in the penultimate stanza Ashbery says: "we put our best foot forward." Clichés reappear with embarrassing regularity throughout the book: "Our worst fears are realized," "a string of successes," "not to worry," "am I my brother's keeper," "anything within reason," "saving face," "getting on famously," "right reason dictates," "the wolf is at the door," and "life is a circus," to take examples from only the first few poems. It is possible to revivify clichés in poetry. In fact, Elias Canetti says that poetry in its essence does precisely that: "truth," he says, "is a reanimation of dying words." And examples of such revivification are easy enough to come by. Robert Creeley's "Old Song" consists almost exclusively of clichés reanimated by the mock-archaic tone; in Alan Dugan's "Last Statement for a Last Oracle," the phrases "You wanted it, / you have it," "living a lie," and "unspeakable condition" are reanimated by the voice of the narrator and by their juxtaposition with inventive formulations; and Philip Larkin's "too good for this life" in "Sunny Prestatyn" is reanimated by irony. Ashbery, though, instead of reinvesting the clichés with meaning, seems simply not to notice their poverty.

Another recurring tic whose first instance appears in "Token Resistance" is Ashbery's habit of using attenuating words. Instead of saying "But made bold / by the rain," he says "But made bold / somehow by the rain." In other poems, he makes a habit of beginning sentences with "Well," as in "Well, anything / within reason, of course," "Well, the upshot of it was," and "Well, let them try it." Analogously, "now," "why," and "oh" make their appearances, as in "Now if there was one thing that could save the situation," "Why, / the very civility that gilded it / is flaking," and "Oh, there is so much to know." Other forms of attenuation, too, permeate the poems (all italics mine): "You, *I suppose*, wanted it this way"; "Then he *sort of* lobbed it / over the fence *if you know what I mean*"; "nobody's nose is to the grindstone / anymore, *I bet*"; "And *you know*, the skunk family approved it too"; "*kind of* puts us out into the middle"; and "I *sort of* long for one of them," to cite a few examples.

Not least, though, of the representative problems in the first poem is the presence of a pseudophilosophical truism: "It / isn't possible to be young anymore." Like the use of cliché, this can be done well. In his short poem "In the Cold House," James Wright successfully makes the banal truism "I am growing old" into poetry by surrounding it with lines that, like a magnifying glass held between a dry leaf and the sun, focus its generality. Carolyn Forché does the same thing for "There is nothing one man will not do to another" in the last line of her poem "The Visitor." The same objective can be accomplished by putting a slight twist on the truism, as W. S. Merwin does repeatedly in "Ballade of Sayings" and Bin Ramke does in "Humiliation of the Aphorism." But Ashbery's bromides remain bromides. "We know nothing about anything," he says, "The future is a ghost," and "Nothing is better than nothing at all." He falls into them often enough to make his title from *Houseboat Days*, "Unctuous Platitudes," into a self-fulfilling prophecy.

I do not mean to exaggerate the case. *And the Stars Were Shining* has its musical passages, its well-conceived images and turns of phrase. For example,

> Say, though,
> that we are not exceptional,
> that, like the curve of a breast above a bodice,
> our parabolas seek and find the light, returning
> from not too far away. Ditto the hours
> we've squandered: daisies, coins of light.

Still, a best-case assessment of this book would make Ashbery a garrulous, minor Eliot who never found the Pound to prune his *Waste Land* or an affected Thomas Wolfe minus the Maxwell Perkins who could make his homeward-looking angel melt with ruth. Ashbery has succumbed to the "creation without toil" that Yeats called "the chief temptation of the artist."

That very absence of toil explains the appeal Ashbery has for the Zeitgeist. After a century of unimaginable evil and unforgivable wrongs, when our collective guilt weighs on us so heavily that we know anything we say is wrong, anything we say will hurt someone (women, children, Native Americans, African Americans, white males, the "physically challenged," the homeless), if we are to say anything we must say nothing, and Ashbery does just that. By using "it" only without an identifiable referent and addressing only a "you" who does not exist, the poems become wholly phatic. ("You, I suppose, wanted it this way / because we all want it this way.") Like the lullaby above the crib or the clock beside the puppy's bed, Ashbery's poems are soporifics, cadence free of any

94

meaning that would interrupt or force us to focus our attention. Video games or sitcoms for the effete, they purpose to pass the time idly and painlessly, to empty brains a century has taught to fear being filled. Ashbery dotes on "The things that happen to other people!" because in an age of electronic isolation, when we are wholly buffered from other humans and from nature by Walkman headphones, faxes, modems, and monitors, he helps us forget that anything could happen to us.

The poems themselves confess their purpose: almost every other poem has a passage that could be an *ars poetica.* "I escaped from the dream of living," he says in "Assertiveness Training," into "a fairy tale with no happy ending, no ending at all, / only bedtime to live ever after." He concludes "William Byrd" by saying: "I can see heaths and coasts; / in them we become magic and empty again." Or, in "Just for Starters":

> I don't know what got me to write this poem
> or any other (I mean, why does one write?),
> unless you spoke to me in my dream
> and I replied to your waking
> and the affair of sleeping and waking began.
> . . . .
> Maybe unimportance isn't such a bad thing after all.

The long title poem includes this especially revealing passage:

> Rummaging through some old poems
> for ideas—surely I must have had some
> once? Some people have an idea a day,
> others millions, still others are condemned
> to spend their life inside an idea, like a
> bubble chamber. And these are probably
> the suspicious ones. Anyway, in poems
> are no ideas. No ideas in things, either. . . .

Some poems, it is true, have no ideas, but *good* poems never lack for them. The ideas may not take an explicit propositional form, but they are present and they *are* ideas. Jan Zwicky's words point out the flaw in Ashbery's malleation of Williams: "The pride with which some artists

announce that they cannot think logically reflects an attitude comple-
mentary to, and as dangerous as, the view that one needs *only* to be able
to think logically." The easiest mistake into which a philosopher can fall
is thought without poetry. Ashbery falls into the easiest mistake for
poets: poetry uninhabited by thought.

The poems in John Ashbery's *And the Stars Were Shining* cast no
shadows. Examples of the aestheticism that renders anaesthetic, they
provide their own epitaph: ". . . there was / no disturbance, nothing to
slide a hand along, / only postscripts. . . ."

Charles Bernstein

In a *New Yorker* article published a few years ago, Richard Preston,
profiling the mathematicians David and Gregory Chudnovsky,
reminds his readers of several facts about pi (which the Chudnovsky
brothers taught their homemade supercomputer to calculate to over
two billion digits). Pi, although a determinate number (as shown by the
possibility of calculating it to so many digits), is not predictable. It
possesses order ("the same digits [appear] in a fixed order forever"),
but not pattern: the Chudnovskys know how to calculate pi to the two
billionth digit but at no point do they know what digit will come up next.
Because it cannot be expressed as a finite algebraic equation, it is called
a "transcendental" number. It can be arrived at only by an infinite chain
of operations. One such infinite chain is "the Leibniz series," which
yields results that "[converge] on pi forever, playing hopscotch over pi
but never landing on pi."

The essays in Charles Bernstein's *A Poetics* are not about math, but
in his treatment poetry resembles pi in several respects. It is transcendental; though ordered, it defies pattern; though determinate, it defies
a finite description; and it announces itself not immediately but
through limits that converge on it. Bernstein's terms for the limits are
"absorption" and "impermeability," and his (infinite) equation is this:
"Translating Zukofsky's formula for poetry / (lower limit, speech; upper
limit, music) / I would suggest that / poetry has as its outer limit, impermeability / & as its inner limit, absorption." Absorption is, roughly,
inclusiveness (of materials to be used by the text, of the reader into the

text, and so on), and impermeability is, roughly, exclusiveness. An example of absorptiveness is that "most diverting of contemporary / absorptive genres, the TV series," because it includes "everyday life" and tries to draw the viewer into itself without impediment. As examples of antiabsorptiveness (a synonym used interchangeably with impermeability), Bernstein cites, among others, the typography in some e. e. cummings poems, and the fragmentation and allusiveness of Pound's *Cantos*, each designed to draw the reader up short, to break the rhythm, to "stun," Bernstein says more than once, quoting Dickinson, "with bolts of melody."

Bernstein uses the terms to enforce several claims. One such claim is that absorptiveness by itself is an unsatisfactory ideal. Such an ideal, as represented by "the 'fourth wall' convention in theater, where what / takes place on stage is assumed to be sealed / off from the audience," only denies the fact that texts are self-consciously "written to be read or heard." Pure absorptiveness, because it "contradict[s the] ever-present other reality through / insulation into a fabricated 'lowest' common / denominator," is "the ideological strategy of mass entertainment, / from bestsellers to TV to 'common voice' poetry." The inevitable result of exaggerating absorptiveness is melodrama.

Bernstein also propounds the claim that antiabsorptive techniques, used well, lead to a more illuminating absorption. Surrealism, for example, uses "antiabsorptive / techniques to reach / [a] 'deeper', more absorbing reality." Unlike the absorption *simpliciter* of mass entertainment, absorption reached through impenetrability can "create a poem that can absorb / its readers in something other than static— / call it ec-static, or u-topia, or say / it is the unnameable that writing constantly / names. To do this requires something strange & jolting." Without absorption the audience cannot gain access to the text, but without antiabsorption the text falls to the criticism George Oppen levels against pop music: it can say only what its audience already believes.

Bernstein argues in favor of unpopularity both in his rhetoric and in his practice of quoting from poets who will never publish with Knopf or sit on the Board of Chancellors of the Academy of American Poets. "To find alternatives to depthlessness," he says, "we must look outside the centers of fashion and promotion—just as we must look outside the

major political parties and major media to find alternative and oppositional political discourses." The result of this unpopular looking outside
will be a multiculturalism of style, without which multiculturalisms of
race and gender remain superficial because the "other" is accommo-
dated only insofar as it resembles the dominant culture.

Poetry, like pi, refuses completion or closure: Bernstein denies
"completed saying," insisting that "poetics . . . is ongoing, . . . and [it]
tries to disrupt or problematize any formulation that seems too final or
preemptively restrictive." Poetry's refusal of closure, like pi's, constitutes its transcendence. "Poetry has the power to absorb . . . other forms
of writing, but these other forms do not have that power over poetry."
"We don't know what 'art' is," any more than we know what pi is, "but we
are forever finding out."

If a single thesis unites a collection of essays the very title of which
(A Poetics) blurs the distinction between singularity and plurality, that
thesis receives its formulation on the penultimate page: "By insisting
that stylistic innovations be recognized not only as alternative aesthetic
conventions but also as alternative social formulations, I am asking that
we bring devices back from a purely structural interpretive hermeneu-
tics." Such a request, like most of the ideas in Bernstein's book, is not
new; we have seen it in, for instance, Hart Crane's "General Aims and
Theories," as we have seen the distrust of pure absorption in Milan
Kundera's definition of kitsch as "categorical agreement with being,"
the argument for antiabsorption as a prologue to absorption in Kant's
aesthetic criterion of disinterest, and the argument for unpopularity in
Rilke's "works of art are of an infinite loneliness." But Bernstein's book
is too wise to be diverted by a desire for mere novelty, as it is too wise to
be swept away by fads, either theoretical or poetic. It is wise enough to
follow its own prescriptions (as in the use, to take an easy example, of
line breaks throughout one essay, which in a book of theory works as an
antiabsorptive technique) and wise enough to meet the objective it
learns from Stein—not to be avant-garde or ahead of its time, but to be
contemporary in Marina Tsvetaeva's sense: "To be a contemporary is to
create one's time, not to reflect it." In its wisdom, A Poetics serves as a
reminder of what theory can be, what poetry is, and what poets must be.

Mark Jarman

Mark Jarman made his bed with *Rebel Angels*, and *Questions for Ecclesiastes* lies in it. Poets help establish the background against which their work will be read and the terms by which it will be judged, whether through their personal lives (Plath), their critical works (Ransom), their political views (Rich), their ecological activities (Snyder), or other means. In Jarman's case, one cannot read *Questions for Ecclesiastes* without recalling the hyperbolic claim, made by Jarman and his coeditor David Mason in *Rebel Angels*, that the "New Formalist" poets "represent nothing less than a revolution, a fundamental change, in the art of poetry as it is practiced in this country."

I have made various public statements of my admiration for the work of Mason, Dana Gioia, Molly Peacock, and Emily Grosholz, and have admired more quietly not only the poetry of Marilyn Hacker, R. S. Gwynn, and other "New Formalist" poets but also the service to the cause of poetry performed by Story Line Press. No one loves a good sonnet sequence more than I do, or a good revolution. But "New Formalism," whatever it is, is no revolution. Except for the odd Ginsberg, Wakoski, or Bly, revered by the untutored hordes begging at the gates, the best-known and most influential poets of recent generations have been "Formalist" poets: Howard Moss at the *New Yorker*, Donald Justice at Iowa, Elizabeth Bishop at Harvard, Stanley Kunitz at Provincetown, Harry Ford's whole cricket team at Knopf. The crown never left the Formalist family. "New" Formalism may be a scheming Gloucester reading his Bible on the balcony, but it is not Liberty leading the people.

Questions for Ecclesiastes assumes the same stance as *Rebel Angels* and succumbs to the same critique. Its title sounds the swagger of Luciferian rebellion, but the book hasn't a recusant bone in its body. It postures as something it is not, and its central sequence, the "Unholy Sonnets," typifies the problem. The sequence opens with this apostrophe:

> Dear God, Our Heavenly Father, Gracious Lord,
> Mother Love and Maker, Light Divine,
> Atomic Fingertip, Cosmic Design,

> First Letter of the Alphabet, Last Word,
> Mutual Satisfaction, Cash Award,
> Auditor Who Approves Our Bottom Line,
> Examiner Who Says That We Are Fine,
> Oasis That All Sands Are Running Toward.

Hardly less holy than the John Donne sequence with which it purports to contrast, this certainly does not one-up the biblical ecclesiast either.

Piety masquerading as rebellion would be less irritating, though, if it were *better* piety. In these sonnets, Jarman's theology bears us no insights, and his language simply cannot match its subject. In the octave just quoted, the stock metaphors, the standard rhymes, and the clunky last three lines, defeated by the form, pale in comparison to similar lists of divine names. Compare Jarman's slack language to the more inventive language of his contemporary, Dana Gioia: "Jeweller of the spiderweb, connoisseur / of autumn's opulence, blade of lightning / harvesting the sky." Or to Hopkins's hard-packed language: "Pride, rose, prince, hero of us, high-priest, / Our heart's charity's hearth's fire, our thought's chivalry's throng's Lord." Jarman's religious verse suffers by comparison not only with Donne and Herbert and Browning and Eliot but with some of his contemporaries: Eric Pankey, for instance, poses more interesting questions for Ecclesiastes and does so with more formal mastery.

My disappointment with the book's theology results not only from its being mundane and expressed in flaccid language but (apologies to Woody Allen) that there is so little of it. This is a book less about God than about the adolescent Jarman, as the narrator announces in the first poem. "Is nothing real but when I was fifteen," the narrator asks. "Is that all I have to write about?" My question exactly. Jarman is not alone in writing about that time of life; it seems almost obligatory today. In another century, though, the manner at least (if not the fact) of our preoccupation with childhood will seem laughable. We so often treat our childhood as a black hole whose infinite gravity draws us ever backward that we forget we have choices and we certainly fail to live up to James Wright's ambition to write "the poetry of a grown man."

Nowadays, when a critical review of one poet by another constitutes a serious breach of professional etiquette, my comments will sound much more strident than I mean them to be. The book has some fine moments, such as "Drought Rain," a beautiful poem that transcends nostalgia for a lost childhood in language as refreshing as its subject.

> . . . these were last night's voices,
> These were the cat-on-screen-door clawings,
> These clear corpuscles, anatomies
> Of visitants, Magi, holy children,
> Entering the sand, slicking cracks
> Like Vaseline, and closing them with mud,
> Exalting and suspending in a dream
> The whole day, making the world
> Of dusty palm leaves, flammable eucalyptus,
> Hiss, rattle, drink up with pleasure.

The title poem, too, is fine, and (unlike the "Unholy Sonnets") *does* generate theological interest and prompt passion. Narrating in the form of questions a visit by a preacher to the parents of a fourteen-year-old girl who has committed suicide violently, the poem dramatizes enough points of view—the preacher, the girl's parents, the narrator in his youth at the time of the events, and the narrator as an adult reflecting on them—that their juxtaposition raises the conflicts that make theological questions important. Spreading that multiplicity of points of view farther might transform this inconsistent, promising book into a consistent and powerful one.

Carl Phillips

No one has the right to be heard. Everyone has the right to speak, and some people deserve to be heard, but to be heard is not a right. The critic who says a poet's voice "demands to be heard" intends that formulation as praise but unwittingly damns its referent. Infants with shit in their diapers demand to be heard, as do toddlers crying for candy in the checkout lane and ballplayers out to milk a few million more from the fools who ante up for season tickets. A voice demands to be heard when it has nothing to offer, when its being heard will benefit no one but itself. Voices with real authority do not demand to be heard. Cassandra did not demand to be heard, nor did Jesus or Gandhi. Meletus demanded to be heard; Socrates did not. The Pope demands to be heard; Mother Theresa did not.

Unfortunately, in our current "culture of complaint," some poets from "underrepresented groups" assume the posture of children and demand to be heard. Instead of asserting the universality of his or her vision, the poet more often begs protection for privative vision. Like so many Somali clans or Serbo-Croat factions, each group (defined by its peculiar combination of race, gender, sexual orientation, or other characteristic) sacrifices the inclusive vision demanded by citizenship for the divisiveness of ethnicity. Most of the proponents of "multiculturalism" have set their sights too low, satisfying themselves with the reservation instead of integration, with welfare instead of work, with the game preserve or zoo instead of ecology. This fundamentally passive position establishes no commonality with anyone outside the tribe except for the shared space of deficiency: we are siblings because we have been abused by the hegemonists.

I do not insinuate that a black lesbian or a gay Native American should try to escape or gloss the peculiarities of her or his viewpoint in order to mimic the socially sanctioned but no less peculiar viewpoint of a white heterosexual male. I do argue, though, that to accept race, gender, and sexual orientation as wholly definitive of one's viewpoint is to implode. Black or white, gay or straight, man or woman, the poet succeeds only by making his or her experience stand for—and stand up to—all experience. Who cannot be Everyperson cannot be a poet.

To be gay or straight, to be a man or a woman, to be African or European or Oriental by descent is in every case to be human, so we need "multiculturalism," but we do *not* need it for the reason usually given: so that all voices will be heard. We need it so that we will not miss important voices due to an arbitrary and irrelevant selection principle. Art is discriminatory. Ceasing to discriminate will benefit no one; learning to discriminate from among the full range of available voices and on a sound basis will benefit everyone.

How, then, does one's vision come to be representative? How did Hamlet become not only a Danish prince but also a representative human being? How does one's voice become larger than oneself? Through the power of language, that mediating presence whose pervasiveness we still imperfectly grasp. Language alone enlarges. The lilt of the language is the volume of the voice. Emily Dickinson deserves to be heard not because she was a woman or a New Englander or a recluse but because "I heard a fly buzz" makes powerful, beautiful, original use of language. T. S. Eliot deserves to be heard not because he was a white Euro-American male but because "The Waste Land" makes powerful, beautiful, original use of language.

The poems in Carl Phillips's *Cortège* stand or fall by the same measure, and he knows it. Phillips is, if the poems' persona resembles his own, a gay African-American man, but he neither capitulates to the white heterosexual male viewpoint nor allows his poems to be circumscribed by his own race, gender, and sexual orientation. The strongest poems in *Cortège* have a force of language that makes his voice universal.

That force of language takes various forms. In "Our Lady" it takes dramatic form. The poem describes a dying drag queen, but with the same mastery of tone that lets works like Thom Gunn's "The Man with Night Sweats" avoid the pathos that infects most AIDS poems. "Our Lady" is Phillips's "To an Athlete Dying Young." The protagonist recollects "the fine gowns that he'd made, just / by wearing them, famous," even as "he lay fanning, / as one might any spent flame, where / it was hot, between his legs." Then "half, it seemed, to remind us, half / himself, he recreated the old shrug" to show off the words "Adore me" tattooed on his shoulder. At that moment:

> it was
> possible to see it, the once
>
> extraordinary beauty, the heated
> grace for which we'd all of us,
> once, so eagerly sought him.

In "I See a Man" (with its echoes of Creeley's "I Know a Man" and Roethke's "I Knew a Woman"), force of language takes the form of precise observation, as the narrator details just what enables him to discern that a man on the sidewalk has just had sex. In "The Man with the Clitoris in His Ear," force assumes the form of indirection. We are never told just who the clitoris-eared man is or why he has this anomaly, but his relation to the speaker becomes clear enough by the final line, in which the narrator whispers into his ear, "*Careful, /* I say *You could do damage, just dreaming.*"

The force in the title sequence is a gestalt. The sequence consists of a prologue, three choruses ("The Viewing," "The Tasting," and "The Dreaming") that alternate with two poems called "Pavilion" and "Interior," and a sonnet as envoi. Each section by itself is enigmatic, operating in the dream logic introduced in this way in the prologue:

> If the sea could dream, and if the sea
> were dreaming now, the dream
> would be the usual one: Of the Flesh.
> The letter written in the dream would go
> something like this: *Forgive me—love, Blue.*

No one of the sections stands complete in itself. As if to complicate the situation, the relation between the sections is never made explicit. Nothing smooths the transition between the catechism-like choruses and the architecturally titled poems that separate them. Yet by the end of the poem, the reader well knows what the cortège is and who the speaker is. The poem ends vividly:

> . . . ignoring the flesh that, burning, gives
> more stink than heat, I dragged what boats I could
> to the shore and piled them severally in a tree-
> less space, and lit a fire that didn't take
> at first—the wood was wet—and then, helped by
> the wind, became a blaze so high the sea
> itself, along with the bodies in it, seemed
> to burn. I watched as each boat fell to flame:
> *Vincent* and *Matthew* and, last, what bore your name.

A reservation accompanies all this praise. *Cortège* is an uneven book. The fragments that compose the prefatory poem, "The Compass," the only poem in the book without capitalization and punctuation, neither give the direction implied by the title nor themselves add up to much. A poem like "Freeze" suffers from a different problem: it is simply too easy. The speaker reflects as he watches moonlight move down his lover's back while the first snow falls. In poems one never watches one's lover's back by the light from one's neighbor's bathroom. In poems it is never the second snow or the fourth. Neither "Youth with Satyr, Both Resting" nor "Seminar: Problems in Renaissance Painting" has enough inventiveness to make itself more than another poem about a work of art. After Keats, an ode on a Grecian urn has to be very good in order not to be bad.

Weak poems are the exception in this volume, though, and its appeal grows with each reading. The strongest poems in *Cortège*, notably the title sequence, have an authority that makes the poet's vision our vision, his experience the experience of all humankind.

Christopher Dewdney

In prefatory comments to a series of short reviews in *Poetry*, Alfred Corn once asserted that the primary function of a review, "positive or negative," is "to *describe* the book in question." Fortunately for reviewers, readers, and the texts themselves, Corn's claim, behind which lurk a Kantian epistemology and a formalist critical ontology, is wrong. Mere description will be inadequate to any good book, since writing aspires precisely to *transcend* description, to be more than any description could capture. A poem suffers in translation as a novel or a play suffers in plot summary. Even when a text recognizes its failure to transcend description, it acknowledges that longing; for example, a mystery novel that does not transcend description simply forbids it: don't tell the ending. In great works the textual elements that lend themselves most readily to description (such as plot) often diminish in importance: novice readers are disappointed to learn that prior knowledge of Ovid's Philomela story told the first audience of *Titus Andronicus* as soon as Lavinia's tongue was cut out that there would be children baked in a pie, but the disappointment occurs only because novice readers don't know where, outside of plot, to look for matter of interest. No review would be intelligible which omitted description, but any review for which description is the telos would insult the text and the reader. The first duty of a book review is to report the results of an encounter with the text in question or (what is perhaps the same thing) to announce possibilities for future encounters.

I mean it as praise, then, that a description of Christopher Dewdney's *Concordat Proviso Ascendant*, no matter how accurate, would be misleading, not only because the book's prose poems are subject to Nemerov's "then they clearly flew instead of fell" problem, but because, like any successful work, the whole exceeds any enumeration of its parts. The enumeration itself is easy enough. The book begins with a "firsthand account of someone who has been *inside* a tornado," because, the note at the end of the book tells us, as "a ritual text," the book "has to be preceded" by such an account. Next comes a poem praising, in *Song of Songs* fashion, various anatomical features of the narrator's beloved, followed by a line drawing, apparently by the author (since it is not credited to anyone else), that looks like a preliminary sketch for a seventies Yes album cover. The majority of the space in this slender volume then goes to a series of seven untitled prose poems. But description does not match encounter.

Concordat's coherence comes from the description at its beginning of a tornado, told in the voice of a high school drama teacher who, with his class, survives a tornado that strikes the school, leaving a bus upside down on the stage where the students had just been rehearsing and the narrator "still picking glass out of [his] scalp two days later." A tornado is brief, violent, and mysterious, and it leaves behind it a long silence. In the book, the tornado functions both as the ruling metaphor, which informs the sexuality of the prose poems, and as the formal paradigm, reflected not only in the individual poems, whose rapid whirling produces violent juxtapositions, but even in the layout of the book, which leaves several silent pages at the end.

Of its function as ruling metaphor, a more precise description would be that, in *Concordat*, the tornado is the vehicle and sex is the tenor. Unlike many poets and most movie producers, though, Dewdney remembers that sex interests only the parties directly involved in it.

Discourse about sex can be interesting, but its interest lies in the discourse, not the sex, and Dewdney's discourse is interesting. Consider this description of the narrator's beloved: "She is liquid darkness occult with desire. An abandoned airplane hangar, scattered curls of corrugated steel littering the floor punctate with sun discs." Such a passage merits inclusion in the long tradition of dissonant praise in poetry, from Homer's "ox-eyed Hera" to Shakespeare's "If snow be white, why then her breasts are dun" to Roethke's "My lizard, my lively writher."

Certainly, Dewdney's discourse has its weak moments. On the page facing the passage just quoted, for instance, this tired passage appears: "By becoming myself I have become someone else. My adoration the natural fulfillment of her sacral narcissism. She is eros displayed. Lank salient grace of her thighs as she consumes me. There is a forest with ferns primaeval down there." Such sentences, though, are the exception rather than the rule. More often the juxtapositions and associations are rapid and musical:

> A single firefly, portentous intermittent star wending silently through the dim canyons of spruce. Meandering green ember in the solid obsidian glass night. A supernumerary planet adding its strange light to the stars. Unearthly machinery of the forest darkness. Nightshade. Low frequency rumble of the planetary surface. The night before the day after. Summer sun a cool furnace in the furthest depths of the moon. The avenues we drive home on. Solstice moon waxing pale in the afternoon sky.

From an insect to the planets to city streets, from evening to night to afternoon, Dewdney in this representative passage takes his readers around the world in eighty words.

In a book that resists description, the first poem, "Litany of Attributes," is a description. It is the only such description in the book, though, as it is the only poem in verse; it functions as a second preface along with the tornado story, separated by the drawing from the poetic sequence that follows. The tone for the rest of the book does not solidify until the first prose poem, which begins the sequence by saying of the narrator's lover that, like the tornado, "She is beyond you now." In Dewdney's book, as in the world, the storm and the silence signify each other but conspire in their refusal to explain.

Jason Sommer

Although the jacket copy on Jason Sommer's *Other People's Troubles* calls attention to the poems' focus on the Holocaust, the poems themselves wisely do not. If the jacket *shouts* Holocaust, the poems *breathe* it with the same combination of urgency and patience that must have been audible on still nights in the bunks of Buchenwald and Birkenau.

Princess Diana's death testifies to how quickly quantity of discourse anaesthetizes us to tragedy. By the third day, who wouldn't flip to *Frasier* rather than endure another news special in praise of the princess? A similar circumstance haunts Holocaust literature. Our Cynthia Ozicks and Elie Wiesels are important, but after half a dozen, who needs another? So much speech has dulled the Holocaust into a counter, a stimulus to which the response is a satisfying sorrow soothed by safe distance and a layer of dust.

Against this background, a body of poems that begins in the Holocaust can be saved from self-indulgence only by becoming as essential as breath. The experiences of Holocaust victims were horrific, as were the consequences for their kin, but to explain those experiences or communicate those consequences calls for an edifice as tightly masoned as *Oedipus*, language as lush as *Lear*. If even the camp guards who created and daily observed those experiences could not *see* them, we who were not there but have heard the stories before will understand them only as other people's troubles unless finely whetted language grafts others' lives into our own.

Just such fruitful surgery does Jason Sommer perform in his evocative, funny, sad, and damn-near-perfect book. "Some distance in," he begins, "a life fills / with people, / despite the early departures," like childhood friends and "the very old / who were at the gatherings once / or twice, tenderly served and seated / to the side, speaking / their other language sparingly / among themselves." Sommer's interest lies in the fact that "of those who vanish forever / you may keep a likeness," and he offers in this book a series of memorable likenesses: Meyer Tsits, for example, "the village idiot of a Munkács neighborhood," whose death ("in 1940 they practiced Holocaust / on his sort just to get the knack") was presaged by the neighborhood children's making fun of him, a reminder to Sommer that "before the astounding / cruelties are the ordinary ones."

Some of the likenesses are of just such ordinary cruelties: the friend "for whom I'd written // a letter of recommendation" who in rush-hour traffic blares her horn and shouts obscenities at the narrator apparently without recognizing him, "tailgating dangerously" in the "rage that can make strangers // out of anyone." The focal likeness, though, is Sommer's Aunt Lilly, a survivor of astounding cruelties, to whom he addresses his portrait of Mengele shitting past a hairball in his colon grown from chewed-off bits of his own mustache. Sommer offers Mengele's unhappiness as a consolation: "a small hell in the body, such as the innocent also experience, / and that hand, which motioned thousands toward death, / those fingers reaching up his ass for years, / this thing I tell you that few people know."

The book's title poem retells a Jewish parable about "the waiting room / where all souls come," each leaving its bundle of troubles hung outside to be picked up after its interview. As in the parable, so in the encounter with Jason Sommer's sagacious book: a soul emerges from its interview surrounded by other people's troubles and better able to bear its own.

Christian Wiman

Poets' voices seldom emerge fully formed: first books more often air promise than plenitude, recklessness than resonance. Christian Wiman's *The Long Home*, winner of the 1998 Nicholas Roerich Prize, speaks with mature authority, not in the voice of a freckled Edward briefly indulged in his babble about the Tower, but of grizzled Odysseus answering Alkinoös while Nausikaa blushes and the Phaiakians forget to feast.

The Long Home starts with a sonnet, "Revenant," that introduces the book's muse, an ancestor of the narrator, one who so loves "the fevered air, the green delirium / in the leaves" and the "storm cloud glut with color like a plum" that she stands in the fields during storms expecting to be struck by lightning, her face "upturned to feel the burn that never came: / that furious insight and the end of pain." But if the storm never speaks *to* her, it does speak *through* her: "spirits spoke through her clearest words, / her sudden eloquent confusion, her trapped eyes."

That prophetic figure in "Revenant" returns as or prefigures Josie, the narrator of the spellbinding title poem with which the book culminates. Obeying the principle implicit in James Merrill's rhetorical question "Who needs the full story of any life?" Wiman's "The Long Home" recounts the crucial events from Josie's rich and dramatic life, beginning with her family's departure from Carolina to a Canaan that (as in the biblical exodus) was really "Papa's dream," and that proved to be Texas, continuing through her sister-in-law's suicide, her own multiple miscarriages, and her husband's death, and ending in a final visit with her grandson back to the farm where she had raised her one son. Wiman develops plot and character as a novel might, but with the concision and repletion of verse.

In between those two poems, Wiman treats the reader to a cluster of lyrics as inviting as a blackberry bramble buzzing in summer with drunk insects, as full of sweetness and scars. A poem like "One Good Eye" exemplifies Wiman's mastery. Its pretext makes it seem least likely to succeed. As Louise Glück's *The Wild Iris* must make plausible poems from an implausible pretext (flowers in the garden speaking), so "One Good Eye" must make a memorable and original poem from a trite pretext (a boy forced to endure the hugs of an ugly aunt). It achieves its unlikely success through the purity and beauty of its music. The poem begins with this melodious sentence:

> Lost in the lush flesh
> of my crannied aunt,
> I felt her smell
> of glycerine, rosewater
> and long enclosure
> enclosing me,
> and held my breath
> until she'd clucked
> and muttered me
> to my reluctant

> unmuttering uncle
> within whose huge
> and pudgy palm
> my own small-boned hand
> was gravely taken,
> shaken, and released.

And ends full circle:

> Then it was time:
> my uncle blundering
> above me, gasping
> tobacco and last
> enticements;
> —while my aunt,
> bleary, tears bright
> in her one good eye,
> fussed and wished
> the day was longer,
> kissed and sloshed
> herself around me,
> a long last hold
> from which I held
> myself back,
> enduring each
> hot, wet breath, each
> laborious beat
> of her heart, thinking
> it would never end.

The sonorous repetition of sounds and the selection of perfect words ("crannied," "clucked," "sloshed") exemplify the musicality that pervades the book.

No one collection commits a poet unalterably to a style or a set of preoccupations, but *The Long Home* already establishes Christian Wiman as a legitimate heir to Frost. The kinship appears unmistakably in a poem like "Clearing," which reanimates the best of Frost's meditative inner-quest poems, such as "Directive" and "After Apple-Picking." But the connection is neither so isolated nor so simple. Wiman is no impersonator among the masses mimicking Frost's mannerisms but a voice possessed of the same rare virtues: independence from poetic fashion, an inviting surface transparency over turbulent depths, shared thematic concerns (home and family, for instance), and an ability to make regional speech representative and individual lives universal. Such exactitude as *The Long Home* embodies, syllable to syllable and line to line, makes Wiman a medium, allows spirits to speak through him, their cadences haunting and their stories true.

Suzanne Noguere

The title poem of Suzanne Noguere's *Whirling Round the Sun* transforms a bus ride through a city in autumn into an epiphany in which "leaf / by leaf turning" serves as "a clue / to earth's revolution." "Whirling Round the Sun" functions as the axis of the collection, and the sense of awe that suffuses the part—"Sometimes it seems almost beyond belief / to be here whirling round the sun"—pervades the whole. Noguere sees every-thing as revelation, not for Augustine's reason but for George Oppen's: the mundane conveys the *mundus* because "Every object includes the universe in its constitution and the laws of its being."

The first section in *Whirling Round the Sun* announces Noguere's ambitions. Ours may be, as Baudrillard suggests, a culture of surface, but that makes Noguere a dissident, insisting defiantly on depth. The first lines of the book's first poem, "Ear Training for Poets," set the tone:

> As the owl in darkness zeroes in
> on the world's small sounds, so must you. But which?
> The deepest comes from any quiet room
> where you can lie down undisturbed. So wait
> and listen.

Drawing on a depth of equal parts introspection and perceptual acuity, Noguere's nuance yields subtle but breathtaking results:

THESCRIBESPACKEDCAPITALSACROSSTHEPAGE
as if they were still chiseling stone until
at last in minuscules they fixed a wedge
of space between the words and a hush fell
upon the page as if light filtered through
trees to a forest floor.

Nearly every page recreates for Noguere's reader that forest-floor hush.

The second section's alnage of family history observes, in her ancestors' sewing and weaving, the unifying force in their sharing of modest domestic work. Noguere describes "Sewing with my Great-Aunt," and talks of the "Extremities" of one of her ancestors: "The doctor calls it *ulnar drift*, the way / your fingers now curve outward on both hands, / the bones driven like snow." She describes "My Grandmother Nellie Braun," who suffered a girlhood fall that left her stooped as short as "her last grandchild at ten," as possessing a spiritual stature far larger than her physical stature: "where she sat was center on each inner map, / with her hands folded in her quiet lap."

In poems about the hands and the brain, and the mysteries of their connection, the third section explores "how the body holds fast to pleasure." That exploration leads inevitably to a series of love poems in the fourth section, irresistible for its range and inventiveness. Some poems use Donne-like conceits, as when Noguere compares her beloved to a saguaro cactus in "Botanical Sketch of You" or compares the lovers to South America and Africa in "Continents": "one hundred / million years do not erode the fit." Another sounds like Hopkins's sprung rhythm: "We Who In / love's circus do love's fireball feat: eat / the witching flames; and lit by our own spotlight eyes vie / who is the better bareback rider." Yet another uses two haiku to woo the lover, "my hermit crab," home to "my lower lips" that mimic "the rose rim of / the pink-mouthed murex."

The final section foregrounds the natural world through which all the preceding poems moved. Its cornerstone poem about the American elm shares the majesty of its subject, but the last poem (a final example of the masterful sonnets sprinkled liberally through the book) completes the whole collection by returning to the maples that appear in the book's first, middle, and last poems. Reiterating the fundamental themes of nature and mortality, the speaker wonders whether "the universe might fall / back upon itself" as the astronomers and the maple leaves seem to agree, or whether "the stars must fly / in one direction only like my life."

In the title poem, "the sparks / fly to my brain with their electric sign / for scarlet, then make my mind a mirror / of amber; and the effort is not mine," but the book, in contrast, represents tireless effort on the author's part. Each poem seems a moment's thought because the book embodies thirty years of stitching and unstitching. The polish of the poems in *Whirling Round the Sun* follows from the fastidiousness its author shares with predecessors like Larkin, Bishop, and Bogan, those who embody Rilke's ideal of "not reckoning and counting, but ripening like the tree which does not force its sap." No elm or maple offers better shade.

Toward a Prodigal Logic

Like words, ideas function only in
combination. *Any* idea by itself
flattens to platitude; only in an
environment that contains its
opposite can it live.

> The eyes' rapid movements fix
> objects in vision, and the mind's
> alternation between contradictory
> ideas settles thought.

Not *my* ideas. Only those I want to
formulate, anatomize, honor. Ideas
I want to overhear as they argue
among themselves.

> Inability to hold more than two
> ideas at once sets the mind's
> horizon, and enforces its
> inevitable failures.

Exactly.

•

Sounds call to other sounds, and
all our treasures stem from their
                    singing.

        Poetry calls insistently for silence,
        as relativity calls for quantum.

Everyone moves word to word
along the path of grammar, but
poets find other paths as well.

        As a grandmaster's every move
        contains those that preceded it and
        those that will follow, a poem's
        every line must contain the whole.

A poem prays to a god it can
neither name nor know.

        Poetry has more important things
        to worry about than truth.

Trust me.

•

We speak through forms, as
mummies preserved in ice or peat
speak through posture.

        Form presumes pattern, but
        originates in resistance to a
        pattern. A spiderweb spun
        between order and chaos, it
        depends on both.

Insatiably demand form, and
restlessly refuse any offered.

        Most settle for faith in what form
        finds. A few insist on the finding.

You figure it out.

•

Con-centration. With or without
an object, thought chooses a
center.

Thought, a fluid, has structure but
not form. Always seeking its level,
it assumes any form its
surroundings offer: rain barrel,
ditch, river, ocean.

Certainly we must arrange
thoughts into sequence based on
legible principles, but we must also
leave them unprincipled and
illegible, in a sequence inscrutable
except as order of occurrence.

Before it is too late.

•

Philosophical questions: their
form says there must be an answer;
their content, that there cannot be.

Responding to one's life, the
world, or god with belief
misunderstands. One does not
believe in a riddle, but tries to find
a solution.

Belief suffocates imagination.

Belief has all the flaws of fidelity,
but none of its virtues.

Though disbelief cannot be
maintained consistently, and
doing so would not constitute
success, any belief still guarantees
failure.

If only.

•

Distance and darkness limit, but
do not impoverish, vision. The
most subtle colors occur at night,
under our more distant stars.

> *Ho skoteinos*. Some of us see better
> in darkness, and trust it more.

Even the blind, sessile anemone
knows the reef with repletion.

> One *learns* to look out a window,
> and one *learns* to look into a soul.
> Including one's own.

Not again.

•

Words separate us from the world
more often than they draw us to it.

> If something other than words did
> exist, words could not speak of it.
> We *can* speak of things other than
> words, but only because they do *not*
> exist. All speech is fictional,
> necessarily.

Simple and elemental may meet
frequently in English, but seldom
in the grammar of the world.

Surely.

•

Temporal order—beginning,
middle, end—achieves meaning
only by representing of other
orders: moral, psychological,
ontological, sacred.

At least one beginning is the
beginning of the end: that immune
deficiency of the spirit that
permits otherwise benign
infections and injuries to grow
unchecked until they kill.

I can name everything I have given
up, and nothing that I have not.

See for yourself.

•

In ideas, too, there are
hunter/gatherers, farmers, and
merchants.

The philosopher who pursues
ideas with enough ardor learns to
distrust the idea of ideas, and
becomes a poet, one pursued by
ideas.

Wait with patience and attention.
The idea you wait for may not pass
by, but another will.

Ideas, wary as wolves, must be
approached from downwind.

Why not?

•

Any pursuit of truth pushes the
pursuer farther from truth, unless a
principle of enforced
randomness in the vehicle (usually
words) saves the pursuer from his
earnestness.

Even those who recognize the
reality in fiction seldom see the
more pervasive, essential fiction in
reality.

Truth: deception in its wholeness,
untainted, replete, and adequate.

Lies we can name, truths we cannot.
Lies that promptly return our calls.

If not.

•

I care less for books I cannot put
down than for those I cannot
forget.

The worth of an enterprise
matches the demand it places on
the media of expression: the trite
can be spoken or shown easily and
often, but depth, by raising
difficulty, renders scarce. That
love prefers it signals poetry's
worth. Love pushes poetry to its
limits, to the edge where it shades
into sentimentality and the edge
where it falls off into nonsense.

Elaborately prolonged foreplay
gives pleasure, and complexly
deferred suicide generates art.

In spite of the evidence.

•

Discoveries occur not from
breaking into thought or
circulating through it, but from
discarding it, leaving it behind.
Thought discloses most after it has
become something else.

Any given fact matters less in itself
than for what it entails for other
facts, the logical possibilities it
opens or closes for them.

Thought, my Moses, leads to a
promised land it may not enter.

Thought, wasteful, vain, and idle,
has no place in the technoculture
of efficiency and profit, and must
become increasingly less visible.

I guess.

•

Strangled by fear, joy, and desire,
reason *is* its bonds.

The most reasonable reject reason,
as the most loving deny love.

One inevitable failure of human
understanding: the mind functions
by substitution (memory for event,
word for thing, name for person),
yet objects worthy of mentation are
sui generis, so no substitute will
work.

Because minds are always hungry,
ideas are never lean enough.

Until.

•

We can only imitate rest, as we can
only imitate hope.

We cannot avoid self-deception,
but we can substitute one
self-deception for another
restlessly and willfully, not
allowing blindness or fatigue to
settle us in one deception.

Only the long, fastidious labor of
tending to its fruition one's most
singular talent forgives the
indulging of one's other,
unexceptional loves.

Nothing is harder than reaching
the river's source. Twenty minutes'
rest undoes an hour's labor, as the
current draws one back to sea.

Of course.

•

That we *arrive* at *conclusions* says all
we need to know about thought.

Reflection. Narcissism inhabits
the very nature of thought.

The collector of ideas treats them
with care but thinks he possesses
them.

Youth spent acquiring ideas can be
completed only by age spent
renouncing them.

A life transformed by ideas must
finally rid itself of them.

Really.

•

Intellectual history as endowment:
others' ideas, the principal,
generate one's own ideas, drawn as
interest.

> The fragility of our ideas: how little
> ours are the principles that select
> and arrange the contents of our
> minds.

Ideas liberate us, yes, but from
other ideas that hold us hostage.

> One idea calls to another, and it is
> the idea that *hears* that matters.

Because.

•

Abundance, in life or art, requires
more than self-knowledge,
self-knowledge more than
reflection, and reflection more
than recounting events.

> Resistance as revelation: the
> rusting weather vane defers to
> necessity, but in a way that
> manifests invisible forces.

Revelation never costs less than
innocence, and often costs more.
The prophets set the price at your
happiness; the tragedians, at life
itself.

Therefore.

•

You know of yourself just what you know of the world, and vice versa.

Any separation between subjective and objective also separates the subjective from itself. Our identity was buried in god's grave.

The attempt to speak of something beyond oneself tells nothing about the referent, but more about oneself than any confession could.

Humans, the animals whose main parasites belong to their own species.

For the courage of one's convictions to count as gain, the courage would have to belong to the convictions themselves, not to the person.

I am the selves I squander no less than those I save.

After the fact.

•

Ideas in the absence of truth, and truth in place of ideas.

We want in ideas what we want in friends: robustness, strength, beauty, depth, generosity.

Unable to lift our hammers and drills, disembodied ideas make nothing happen, but it is disembodied ideas that haunt us.

Ideas have force *because* they are unhindered by reality.

I'll deny it.

•

The larynx is not the only vehicle
of voice, nor language its sole
medium. Think of clay-encrusted
hands, and pots fresh from the kiln.

Illiterate souls, illegible lives, and
their inaudible cries.

The will to impose one's god on
others derives from a too-limited
concept of god, and the discovery
of a doctrine in a text from not
understanding the power of words.

Many manifestos, one at a time,
manufactured of one's most urgent
disbeliefs.

Salubrious illumination comes
always from some sun outside the
hothouse.

You wish.

•

Faith: the time lag between
falsification and renunciation.

Faith satisfies itself with
something said. Doubt finds new
ways to say it.

Faith perverts the intelligence,
finalizing preliminary aims.

Prejudice is bad not because it is
false but because it expresses a
failure of the imagination. Accept
received fictions, or create new
ones through imagination's
attentive encounter with the world.

Never.

•

What do you mean, the idea *in* a
play or *behind* a poem?

> Poetry in place of health, or as the
> rare bloom sustained by perfect
> health.

Poetry, vital to the oppressed, dies
of decoration elsewhere. The
parrot's colors still flame in the
cage, but to different effect.

> To resemble no other, a poem risks
> not being a poem.

Suppose stories merit telling but
poetry opposes plot. How will a
poem, born to Leah, justify its own
existence?

> Can any poem atone for its mortal
> sin of being a poem?

Never, never, never.

•

No deep thoughts, only single
chisel strokes. Nor does depth
accumulate with the slivers, but
reveals itself as and through the
created form.

> Like a melody or mathematical
> pattern, a shape is a thought.
> Bach's "Lute Suites" do not convey
> an idea, they are one. So for the
> pyramids, the Parthenon,
> Vermeer's "Lacemaker."

126

Thought rejects the form that
claims to own it for the form it
            claims to own.

            I told you so.

                        •

                        An ancient artifact (a prehistoric
                        bone tool, a twenty-year-old film)
                        tells a history, but not the one that
                        led up to it: anything not already
                        known about that history it keeps
                        secret. It tells instead the history—
                        entire—of what came after it: the
                        history of its medium, the demise
                        of the culture that created it and
                        the origin of ours, even when we
                        thought its culture *was* ours.

History began with us, history led
    to us, history will end with us.
    Three masks for one mistake.

                        The past loses its meaning as soon
                        as the future is over.

Time repeats one word endlessly
    but forever varies its meaning.

                        Civilization: the agreement
                        humans make to be crueler to each
                        other than nature is to us.

It's not that the sins of the father
find the son, but that the sins of
    the son are his search for the
                        father.

            Count on it.

                        •

New ideas *are* dangerous, not
because they corrupt old beliefs,
but because they *become* old
beliefs, narcissistically completing
and justifying themselves through
argument, instead of humbly
replacing themselves.

Accuracy and permanence in an
idea are less useful standards than
the inevitability with which the
idea must be left behind.

Ideas assume direction and gather
force as they age, but they also
become harder to steer.

We recognize ideas as disease only
after infection.

I saw it myself.

•

Depth of character matches the
tension of one's internal dialogue.

Any equivalence between
intelligence and virtue would
reside in the opposition between a
rich capacity for "as if" and an
intuitive, binding recognition of
"not so."

An education that transforms
fortuitous to deliberate character
also fosters moral snobbery and
demands that humility, no longer
natural, be restored by the will.

Dialogue defers violence best when
backed by a threat of violence.

Underwater.

•

Thought has always been difficult.
Why do so few still try?

Slug trails crisscrossing the
sidewalk in morning sun: we see
the results of thought, not thought
itself.

Thought like a hotel room: three
walls of cinder block and one of
windows, giving one view, of the
dirty air over flat roofs and
freeways.

She promised me.

•

One cannot anticipate a
metaphor's effect on either term.

Any optometrist can measure the
accuracy of literal vision, but
nothing numbers the extent of
one's metaphorical blindness.

Can we resist the temptation to
transform mysteries into truths?

What is true remains so by being
left out of all accounts.

Truth: not itself but love. Love: not
itself but truth. It must be so. How
could that which transforms our
identity be self-identical?

What costs more, truth or its lack?
How would we know? And why
would we want to?

Except.

•

Ill will makes me mean. A small
vocabulary makes me dangerous.

Words act as ambassadors less
often than as wards or terrorists.

The liar will trip on his own words,
but not because language is just.
Language, that prankster, that
hyperactive boy, trips the truth-
teller, too.

All poetic problems link to
language that cannot lift its own
weight.

I tried to stop.

•

Metaphysicians talk about what we
perceive only through its effect on
other things (wind on trees, the
gods on our lives), but they talk as
if we perceived it directly, as if,
indeed, we could perceive *anything*
directly, and perception were not
itself one of those "other things."

We say so much because there are
so many things we want not to
hear.

Halve the proof and triple the tale.

He wouldn't listen.

•

130

Ideas like sniper fire. Ideas like
melody that makes the buds in the
rosette bloom.

Ideas may accompany moral
change and amplify it and make
the subject aware of it, but they
cannot cause it.

Ideas themselves matter to history
less than do their distortions.

An idea—*any* idea—isolates one
absolutely.

Ideas contain their own
contradictions *and* their own
suicides.

Who knows?

•

A few ascensions inform and
energize the intervals between.

The marasmus named *nostalgia*
occurs when affection for some
past self overcomes the will to
create a new one.

Approximating uniqueness pulls a
person past others'
comprehension, as approaching
the speed of light takes objects out
of our sensory range.

To each some calling comes, but its
echoes in the surrounding
mountains make the chosen one
determine her own direction to
follow it.

Take it back.

•

Noncontradiction, self-identity:
  necessary fictions, but fictions.
               Self-understanding would be
               easier if we were self-identical.
Our finitude: we can trade one self
  for another, but not trade back.
               Discovering one's identity only
               prompts the more difficult task
               that follows: a renewal such that
               one's identity must be
               *re*discovered. Any identity fixed
               long enough for
               self-understanding to catch up
               needs transformation.

I said take it back.

•

For once the passive voice reveals
something, the active voice hides.
    That no one can have done the
      calling does not preclude my
having been called, my own beliefs
    and my own will be damned.
               "The groundlessness of our
               believing" draws beliefs past hope
               of harbor, abandons them,
               restless, at sea.

You're just wrong.

•

The illness we name experience,
the character flaw we call thought.

> Thought's erratic flight: better
> butterfly than bird.

Preparation for thought packs the
mind as tightly as it can with
words. Thought itself clears one
small space and listens to what
words rush in to fill it.

> Abstraction reveals the world
> because form is thought.

To the artist who finds a new form,
her medium will reveal the world.

> I want to find a poetic form as
> fecund as tempered tuning, as
> subtle and revealing, as rational, as
> replete with possibilities for
> beauty, as inexhaustible.

•

To attain absolute subjection, where obedience and rebellion are twins; not the mind's fullness, but its most meticulously prepared emptiness. / To hear not the words that have been spoken, but those that should have been. / To locate the trail of the thought that must not be thought, and pursue it to my death. / To balance the courage to follow my instincts with the wisdom not to, my desire for transcendence with unstinting love of the mundane. / To bear the burdens of omniscience though I know nothing. / To make my will, itself part of the world, stronger than the world.

To know once for all what I cannot do, but never quite to know what I can. / To do well what a simple recursive machine could not do better. / Never to underestimate the transformative power of defeat. / To attend, as one who longs for rain watches the sky and listens for distant thunder. / To be responsive but irresponsible. / To be drawn by something inarticulate but precise, as homing pigeons and salmon and sea turtles are drawn by magnetism and the seasons and their own bodies.

Not to be content with one falsehood but to gather many. / Not to avoid lying to others or to myself, but to permit myself only lies that underwrite renewal, that reveal lies as lies. / To renounce, now and often, all that I have said before, and to say not only what must be said but also what must be unsaid. / Not to fall into nihilism but to dive. / To trust my mind as I trust my bones: completely, irrevocably, joyfully, fearfully, intensely. / To defy sense, in fulfillment of a commitment to clarity. / To find a place I recognize but cannot name, another world identical to our own, a place so strange and disorienting that there my life must begin again.

To account for each hour *because* life cannot but be wasted. / To fish some life daily from the void. / To extend indefinitely the lag between lightning and thunder. / To accept that there is no speaker but never that there is no spoken. / To hear the work that calls for my life, though it may not have the loudest voice. / To follow god into the desert, form deep into the caves, though no one will find my papyrus or my paintings for five thousand years.

To attain modesty by sacrificing humility along with vanity. / To master my desires not by subduing them but by elevating them. / To live a melody line or, better, a chord progression or counterpoint. / Not to let love's blurred edges prevent its achieving direction. / To muster patience enough to wait at the base of the tree until the prey falls. / To ask philosophical questions without philosophical method. / To have one idea, any idea, often enough to get it right.

•

The vices, including art, share
presumption as their precondition.
Pharisees and poets: even god
ought to treasure my work.

Sins of the artist: obsession with
one object of attention,
impatience, self-absorption,
grandiose ambition, restlessness.
Virtues of the artist: obsession
with one object of attention,
impatience, self-absorption,
grandiose ambition, restlessness.

Blithe and egoistic volubility starts
the poem, fastidious and
self-condemning concision
completes it, presumption
publishes it.

Never mind.

•

Ideas matter less when one
understands them than when one
does not.

An important idea can be begun
but not completed. Stronger in its
second form, weaker in its third.

Ideas come from words but can be
poisoned by corrupt perceptions.

Attention creates the void out of
which ideas are drawn.

Ideas like lovers demand the
attention of one's whole body, and
must be seduced. The winning
costs one's life.

I would have.

•

The long labor of construction
prevents fewer people from
building reflective lives than does
fear of the demolition that
precedes and prepares for it.

Though we never cross the divide,
the manner of our trying may
mean life or death to those looking
at us from the other side.

Ambition: only so many trailers
before you start losing speed.

Sooner.

•

Only absolute obsession
incorporates its opposite,
transforms into itself even denials
and attempts to escape.

Eyes follow movement
automatically, and reflexes force
fingers to flee heat. The faculty of
attention I wish to heighten starts
with *resistance* to attention.

In a robust attention, even
distractions would increase its
focus.

Otherwise.

•

Ideas as gems whose facets will
flash in the light, yes, but also as
journeys that cannot be
photographed or condensed.

Intellectual dramas are tragic,
because all ideas come to grief.

An explanation of an idea is a
different idea.

People sometimes fail to
understand the ideas of others, but
more often they fail to understand
the consequences of their own
ideas.

I won't do it.

•

The hold of religion: *nothing* is
stronger than the will to untruth.

A little anthropology in religion, a
little science or history. The
fundamentalists are right:
eventually the one grain of sand
will make one take off the shoe.

The names of ideas in preference
to ideas themselves.

Another St. Peter's of Popsicle
sticks.

This is not my fault.

•

Virtues vary in a life as seasons in a
year.

> Seven numbers in short-term
> memory, six words as moral ideals.

Virtue died not from nihilism but
from pleonasm, not from the
world's being empty of value but
from its being all too full.

> *Cogent* dissent. Habitual rebellion
> is a posture.

Courage fails through timidity or
foolhardiness, genius through
normalcy or idiocy. Better the
latter forms.

> Moderation: a mean between
> extremes or a conjunction of them.

I can't believe it.

•

As narrative needs plot but settles
for spectacle, so reason falls for
coherences instead of the scissions
it needs.

> The mind must multiply its
> contradictory instincts and
> actions: hoard and spend, burrow
> and survey, hide and seek, obey
> and overthrow.

Reason calls for its own head, and
only a naive unreason could think
itself reasonable for consistently
pursuing reason.

Regardless.

•

Like tags on a dog's collar, words'
sounds show the sentence's
movement. Meaning in language
receives too much attention;
music, too little.

If philosophers seek to discover
words' laws and grammarians to
obey them, poets seek to violate
them.

We created language to express not
our knowledge but our doubts.

Oh, come on.

•

Between the teleology we long for
and the world's purposelessness
stands a gap hope and happiness
deny, that poetry tries to name.

Because we perceive meaning only
through restrictions of scale—
under the aspect of eternity
neither my life nor my death
matters—artists fear historical
perspective, which clarifies one's
inconsequence. Only with
particular courage can one face the
past of one's art, that mirror that
reflects one so unambiguously as
zero.

Under no circumstances.

•

Only new syntax conveys old
truths. Words must argue among
themselves.

For every two parts information,
truth needs three parts invention.

Truth: an idea we can formulate
but not comprehend, a liquid we
can skim across, suspended only
by surface tension, prey from
above or below.

Perfect clarity—music—defies the
understanding perfectly. It does
not tempt one into belief, and
cannot fall victim to truth.

Undoubtedly.

•

Not whether we can discover (or
posit) order, but what *method* of
discovery will make that order
most replete.

Even the most focused attention is
already abstraction, has already
drawn the object out of its
surroundings into one's own.
*Per*ceptual space cannot be
separated from *con*ceptual.

Abstraction can remove one from
perception, or take one farther in.

Nevertheless.

•

Love springs from the basest
possible motives, and must be
made noble.

In this indifferent universe, love,
like justice, must defy truth.

The rule of law that prevents
caprice and terror also prevents
love. A civil world, were one
possible, would be loveless.

Recognition of one's own mortality
manifests itself as love. Denials of
mortality dissipate bonds of love.

Though we build our rites around
them, vows only announce a
background of promise that could
never be enacted ritually. Vows bob
on the surface. Promise is to love
what depth is to the sea.

Love depends less on passion than
on respect, and (like all other arts)
less on strength of will than on its
endurance.

Correct me if I'm wrong.

•

Moral principles, grammatical
principles: lives, like sentences,
have pitch and rhythm, are in tune
or out, though in lives anacoluthon
in one can terminate another.

Not to *follow* principles repeatedly
(too easy, too safe) but to choose or
invent principles over and over.

Looking across the abyss between
principle and application, one
hears loose stones fall down the
cliff face but hit no river below.

Between the rule and the instance
we hang, metal between magnets.

Not here. Not anywhere.

•

In relation to others we find the
distances within ourselves.

People abandon universality as an
ideal when they misunderstand it
as the elevation of particulars to
universality rather than an infinite
ability to make itself particular.

A voice becomes public not
through publicity—turning the
most heads, an ambition poets
should leave to Hollywood—but
through the richest reciprocity
between one individual spirit and
the human collective.

Overwhelmingly.

•

The artist paints or composes or
writes from necessity, without
knowing it *as* necessity, and
therefore without relief from fear
and self-doubt and the demand for
constantly renewed decision.

Whatever other writers ask of their
readers—identification with a
protagonist, willing suspension of
disbelief—poets ask for an act of
imagination equal to their own.

For every philosopher who praises
sound decisions, two poets
celebrate unsound ones.

It is hard *not* to say what you mean,
though the poet must try.

Categorically.

•

The specialized knowledge that
gave a few people the moon
exacted from the rest of us the
stars, about which any illiterate
ancient shepherd knew more than
we.

The mass media provoke increased
reliance on dramas with no
ending: markets, politics, weather.
But the drama we ourselves enact
remains the same: a single, short
human life, with its very definite
end.

Try to stop me.

•

Philosophy: ideas without lust,
anorexic ideas that wish to be rid
of the body. Poetry: willful ideas,
bulimic, overrun by the body.
Either way, thought is fatal.

An *un*satisfied hunger may stay
away longer, but extended absence
will make its return more vindictive.

Anorexia. Mastery of desire may
not be mastery.

Deep thought: hunting a tiger. You
can prepare to meet an idea, you
can go where they live, but you can
never be sure of finding one. Nor
can you avoid danger: thought may
surprise you, and ideas can kill.

Thought: a stare-down against
nihilism. The first to blink loses.

I thought we'd settled that long ago.

•

One who knows the sound of god's
voice can hear only the voice he
expects. One who does not know
god's voice cannot distinguish it
from others.

God, soul, love. Things that cannot
themselves be, but without which
we could not be.

God's silence *is* a commandment.

God's absence makes my defiance
identical to my praise.

I'm waiting.

•

Defenders of the truth believe in
truths that need defense.

The degree of the damage
determines which lies one
mistakes for truths. The nature of
the damage determines which lies
one loves as lies.

Human expression depends on,
but is falsified by, hope. The truth
could find expression only if it
could be purified of all hope.

No search for truth can be more
adequate than its accompanying
self-doubt is overwhelming.

I'm still waiting.

•

Accurate self-assessment threatens
society and heals oneself.

Haste seduces us into scanning the
sky, not observing the earth.

The mass media mimic our senses'
responsiveness to change, but what
replicates our capacity to attend to
what endures?

The urge to account for our
perceptions and desires perverts
them.

We come bearing prejudices like
useless gifts to the infant king.

Easy to trust the voice in one's head,
hard to make it worthy of trust.

Hold on.

•

No place words cannot lead, and
no place they *will* not lead.

Some words lead into the open,
some down into a cave.

Poets lament the incapacity of
words, their smallness before
experience, in denial of the real
problem, our own minority, our
inability to fill the capaciousness
of language.

Our attention flags, but the
language is never exhausted.

Don't interrupt me again.

•

The purer a poet's privacy, the
longer the poems will take to find
their audience, and the more
profoundly they will speak to it.

There are *only* minor prophets. To be
heard more widely one would need
to commit the popular sins against
which prophets are called to speak.

Between what you know and what
the work knows, the wilderness
that knows you.

Philosophers who leave the body
behind resent poets for bringing
the body along on the soul's
journey.

The body, too, imagines. It haunts
the chimneys of the exiled gods.

Poems emerge alive from memory
like ghosts from purgatory.

Absolutely.

•

Beauty, no passive quality, does not inhere, but is *asserted*.

Purer than excess balance may be, but less beautiful.

Beauty thrives, like anaerobic bacteria or ocean-floor tube worms, even in the absence of apparent preconditions for life.

"Eye contact." Nothing touches more profoundly than the intangible.

Suddenly. Quite suddenly.

•

The fewer and more consistent our ideas, the more we mimic automatons. Our animation occurs when they multiply and rave and contest each other ceaselessly.

Keeping commitments is difficult, and demands determination. Honoring commitments is contradictory, and impossible.

Many occasions demand that we go against our better judgment.

Even when it is easy to arrive at the end, it may be hard to recognize the end *as* the end.

The number of ideas one has matters more than which ones they are.

Even sound ideas must be perpetually renewed, or rot.

Repetition will not make an idea
sound; constant variation might.

A reflective person wills to
maintain more ideas than she
needs.

Oh.

•

The mind suffers from trust in its
own capacities.

Minds like stars stay suspended in
space by attraction to other stars.

An urban conceptual space—a
densely populated mind—permits
congress between ideas, but risks
forgetting that food, even spiritual
food, remains organic, and still
comes from the farm.

A life of the mind dredges a
reservoir on which to draw in
drought.

A mind free enough to flit bud to
bud learning new dances like bees,
but bound to bring back pollen for
the hive to translate into honey.